first foal

First foal

Jane van Lennep

J. A. Allen
London

British Library Cataloguing in Publication Data
van Lennep, Jane
   First foal.
   1. Horses. Breeding
   I. Title
   636.1082

   ISBN 0-85131-532-1

Published in Great Britain in 1991 by
J.A. Allen & Company Limited,
1, Lower Grosvenor Place,
Buckingham Palace Road,
London, SW1W OEL

Reprinted 1994

Typeset in Hong Kong by Setrite Typesetters Ltd.
Printed in Hong Kong by Dah Hua Printing Press
   Co. Ltd.
Colour processing by Tenon & Polett Colour
   Scanning Ltd., Hong Kong

Designed by Nancy Lawrence

CONTENTS

INTRODUCTION

An estimated 45 per cent of all foals (including Thoroughbreds) are bred by owners who breed from only one mare. Most of these caring owners want to do the very best for their mare and foal, but have little past experience to guide them through the hazardous course to producing a healthy youngster. Much very technical information is available, of course, but this is perhaps more appropriate for vets or large-scale professional breeders. This book offers all the essential information in a factual, practical and easy-to-read style. It is as relevant to the small-stud owner as to the one-mare owner it is primarily written for, and is based on a solid foundation of personal experience. Students and trainees will find it invaluable reading.

The text is illustrated with many photographs (including several of the author's own photographs) intended to show salient points clearly and also to retain the beauty of foaling amid the stark realities of technology and science so often portrayed in practical manuals of stock breeding.

The vet's role has not been diminished by overdetailing diseases and problems, but, rather, normality has been emphasised and the role of the owner enhanced.

Having your foal at home can be rewarding for all the family, but do not spoil the foal. Owner Kim Burns with Bess and the children. The part-bred Arab foal was born palomino, but, like her dam, will go grey. Bess is wearing a fly veil.

DEDICATION

This book is dedicated to the Thursday evening class who assured me it was needed and nagged me into writing it.

AUTHOR'S NOTE

Every care has been taken to ensure that all the information contained in this book is correct. If there are any errors or omissions, they are entirely the responsibility of the author.

1. WHY BREED A FOAL?

There are very many reasons why people who are not professional horse breeders decide to breed. It usually starts because a much-loved mare is no longer able to work under saddle, but could perhaps produce a foal. If a good mare becomes incapacitated, say, due to an accident and through no fault of her own, then breeding from her could be practical. If, however, the truth is that after years of struggling with her uncertain temperament, and your own fading nerves, you have decided to breed rather than face parting with her, then it is not a good idea. Never breed for profit. Breeding horses is a good way to lose money, but rarely to make it. Even professional breeders are in the habit of making a loss. Around 20,000 Thoroughbred mares produce 10,000 potential race horses per year. Half of these make it to the training yards, and not all of them, by a long way, will ever make it to a race track. Only one will win the Derby. Most 'retire' before they are four years old.

It is a good idea to frighten yourself with some costings before you start. The mare's keep has to be considered, as well as that of the foal. She should be up to date with her vaccinations, and should be swabbed before going to the stud — vet's visit plus consultation and advice, the swab, postage, lab fees — see how it adds up? There will be keep charges and probably more vet's fees at the stud, as well, of course, as the stallion's covering fee. Check if this carries VAT — it comes as a nasty shock if you are not expecting it. Some stallion owners may want a second payment in October if the mare is definitely in foal. Again, check all of this before committing yourself.

Zorya (Arab) enjoys some winter sun, a bite of grass and an expanding belly. She has $3\frac{1}{2}$ months to go before the birth of her first foal.

I

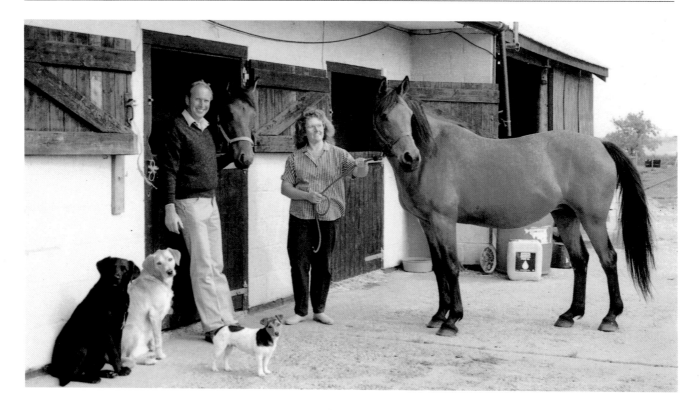

(*Above*) Happy families! Terri and Stuart Goulding with Serenity and her yearling (their first home-bred foal) and friends. The pleasure of breeding from your own mare.

(*Opposite*) Long legs get in the way of grazing. It is better if foals do not go out wearing a foal slip in case it gets caught on something. Foals also, as in this case, outgrow their foal slips extremely fast.

Regular worming (every six weeks or every four if your pasture is not regularly rested) is vital.

Fortunately, in-foal mares usually 'do' well and will not cost more to feed until the last three months. You may find your insurance bill goes up, however. Get a quote from the vet for night visits in case he or she is needed at foaling. Find out how much foal registration fees will be and whether or not you need to join any breed society. Unregistered foals could be worth less and may not be worth breeding for sale. You may need a bigger stable, safer fencing and a stock of supplies for foaling emergencies — such as bottles, teats, a foal rug and replacement milk powder.

Do your sums first, then the shock will not be too great later. Never look on a foal as a 'free bonus' and remember that, as in all things in life, you get what you pay for. Higher stud fees tend to produce more valuable foals.

If you cannot afford to become a breeder, forget it now.

2. THE MARE

So you think you are rich enough to carry on. Congratulations! You are on the way to one of the most rewarding experiences of your life. However, you must be very honest when looking at your mare, because dubious mares breed dubious foals.

Good temperament is vital. Your foal will be in her company for many months, and will be very much influenced by its dam's temperament and behaviour. Cross, aggressive mares often rear like-minded foals. Mares that cannot be caught teach their foals to dodge humans too. All stable vices, such as cribbing or weaving, are best avoided. Never, ever, breed from a mare that has given you any cause to fear her in the stable. The ideal broodmare should like people, be tolerant of all manner of handling, and be sociable with other horses. She should be viceless and willing.

Soundness is also very important. Ideally, a broodmare will have proven herself under saddle — a test of temperament as well as soundness. Unsoundness which could be due to hereditary factors would be a good reason for rejecting the mare. Certain types of conformation can predispose a horse to the development of diseases or problems such as navicular disease, ringbone, spavin, whistling or roaring. Wobbler syndrome may be inherited. If your mare has a problem and you are not sure if it could be passed on, then talk to your vet. Conformation is highly inheritable and faults such as very sloping pasterns and small joints, which increases susceptibility to joint, tendon and ligament injuries, should be looked at very critically. Any unsoundness should be fully checked out, to convince yourself that not even the possible *tendency* to develop that unsoundness is likely to be passed on.

(*Right and below*) The charm and cheekiness of young foals.

Conformation also affects the future ride and look of the horse, as well as its soundness. If not really bad, certain conformational faults need not bar a mare from breeding but it is important to be aware of them in order to make sure the stallion you choose is strong in the areas where the mare is weak. In this way, many faults can be corrected.

Long, dippy backs can cause problems depending on the extent of the dip. An inexperienced breeder should consult a vet or an experienced breeder for advice on whether or not their dipped-back mare would be suitable for breeding. If the back dips, it is likely that the uterus does too, and therefore it will not drain well after foaling. Dippy-backed mares are thus more prone to infections and can be difficult to get in foal, especially if they also have poor perineal conformation. The anus should be immediately above the vulva and in the same plane. If it is sunken, with the vulva curving out below it, the chances are that the mare will have an infection that is difficult to clear, as droppings will have contaminated the vulva. In addition, a mare with this conformation may suck air in through the vulva, which increases the risk of infection. Poor vulval conformation may benefit from Caslick's operation; a minor operation performed under local anaesthetic which lessens the chances of infection, and improves the chances of conception. Again, the vet should be consulted on this matter. She may be difficult to cover and may be an unthrifty mare, hard to keep in good condition — it is often severe weight loss, past or present, that sets off this kind of conformation.

A broodmare needs to be roomy, with a good barrel, plenty of length from hip to hock, and sufficient width in the pelvis for foaling to be trouble-free. Mares with a tendency to filled legs will suffer more when in foal, particularly during the last few weeks of pregnancy. You may not want to risk breeding from such a mare, especially if she is getting on in years.

There is a lot of debate about the age at which it is reasonable to begin a mare's breeding career. It must be sensible to delay breeding until the mare has had a chance to prove herself as a sound, willing ride. Although biologically capable of getting in foal at two years old (or even younger) most breed registers bar foals that were conceived when either parent was under 24 months. Even professional studs do not make a regular practice of covering mares that are under four years old.

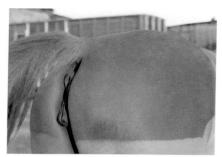

(*Above*) Good perineal conformation is important in a broodmare.

(*Left*) These mares are 6–7 months into their pregnancies. Their big bellies are lower at the widest point than would usually be the case if they were just fat.

(*Above, right and opposite below*)
Happy, healthy mares and foals.

The 'average' broodmare then has an 'average' of one foal every two years until she is 14 years old or so — the average age when she completes her duties. Should you wish to continue using your mare as a broodmare, you may be advised to put her in foal every year because some believe that this actually makes it easier for a mare to conceive. Some mares (the exception rather than the rule) will go on breeding into their twenties.

If a mare is fit and healthy, with a normal oestrous cycle, there is no reason to suppose she will have problems in foaling, but it seems fair to suggest that teenage mares be checked out by a vet before you start working out names for the as-yet unconceived foal. Sound, healthy mares tend to have sound, healthy foals, whatever their age. Many mares have foals in their teens, often because their competitive or working life finishes and having foals becomes their next career. Unlike people, mares do not have a menopause, although fertility does decline considerably with age.

SOME REASONS FOR NON-PRODUCTION IN MARES

1 Mare not covered — did not come into season;
                     — owner's decision not to cover;
                     — would not stand for the stallion;
                     — vet's advice (injury, disease, age).
2 Mare covered at the wrong time.
3 Stallion infertile.
4 Mare temporarily infertile — infection;
                          — overweight;
                          — underweight.
5 Mare permanently barren.
6 Mare conceived but the foal was lost — hormone deficiencies;
                               — infection;
                               — foal defects;
                               — accident.
7 Foal born dead — infection;
                     — congenital defects;
                     — malpresentation.
8 Foal died since birth — congenital defects;
                         — accident;
                         — nervous defects;
                         — infection;
                         — inherited defects.

(*Above*) First day out for Tracker aged 1 day. A small, safe paddock like this is ideal. Shahala (Arab) wears a tail bandage to keep her tail clean. Never leave a mare and foal unattended at this stage. The tail bandage was taken off that evening.

3. CHOOSING A STALLION

Collect as much information as you can before you start looking at stallions. If some things are very important to you, such as type, colour, breed, size or ability, then certain stallions can be ruled out. You can only get a good foal by putting a good mare to a good stallion. Be very clear about what failings the mare has and what criteria in the stallion are especially important. Breeding is a lottery of genes, and you do not know in advance what hand Lady Luck will deal you, but if you limit yourself at first to mature, established stallions with plenty of progeny, you can get some idea of the type of stock he will produce. A young stallion is always a bit more of a gamble.

(*Opposite*) Cross-bred mare bred to Arab stallion Triumphal Chant. Star with foal, Tammy.

(*Left*) Triumphal Chant (Arab), British National Champion 1986. A good stallion can improve all types of stock, providing the mares are basically sound.

Welsh mare and foal.

In the absence of any other information, your foal should mature at the average of its parents' heights. Geldings often gain another inch. First foals can be smaller than subsequent ones. Big-bodied mares will produce bigger foals than mean-bodied, herring-gutted mares. Some stallions consistently produce big foals and others seem to sire only small models. What a stallion produces is more important than what he looks like himself, so look at as much of his stock as you can and let them make up your mind for you. Like the mare, the stallion must be sound, well made and good tempered. It is advisable for the amateur breeder to use a licensed stallion although some breeds do not require a licence. Older stallions may have a Ministry of Agriculture, Fisheries and Food licence; most, however, now have a breed society licence, issued by their breed society following successful veterinary examination and, in some cases, blood typing to confirm the breeding and identity. Make sure his progeny are eligible for registration.

People often wish to try to breed a foal that will mature bigger than its dam. I do not think it is fair to use a stallion over two hands taller than the dam; there are plenty of horses

around that are the result of such very 'mixed marriages', but the mare could easily have serious problems, so, if adding a lot of height, it is best to avoid trying to add a lot of substance as well. A show hack is unlikely to breed a heavyweight hunter, so putting a big Irish Draught over a small hack may not yield the desired results; the height of one and the bone of the other may not create your ideal! There is also the added risk that a big stallion can seriously and permanently damage a small mare at covering.

Types rather than breeds are often the result of crossing different breeds. On the European continent, so-called warmbloods are the result of crossing draught, carriage, Thoroughbred and Arab to create a type, then breeding within that type to create a breed. In the UK it is more traditional to use pure-bred stallions, often Thoroughbreds, on native, heavy or first-cross mares to produce a type. Traditionally, the colts are all gelded, so we have to keep starting again. An exception is the British riding pony where good colts have been kept to produce a quality pony of distinct type. The 'originals' were the result of putting small Thoroughbred stallions to mares that were produced by crossing Arabs with native ponies. Nowadays, one has to go back several generations to find a Thoroughbred stallion or to identify the strain of Arab blood. By introducing more native blood, ponies of show hunter type can be produced.

(*Above left*) Thoroughbred mare and foal. (*Above right*) Arab mare and foal.

All three foals on these pages turned grey, having been born a dark shade of the colour they would have been had they not been grey, i.e. black, bay and liver chestnut.

Hacks are often Thoroughbreds that did not make the grade on the racecourse, Anglo Arabs (Arab and Thoroughbred blood), overgrown riding ponies or perhaps a cross between any of these. It is said that hacks, and cobs for that matter, 'happen' and cannot be bred, but it is interesting to look at the breeding information given of, say, hacks, at a large show, where you will notice several sharing the same sire. That stallion is obviously promising for siring a show hack from a suitable mare. Show cobs often have a lot of Irish Draught, perhaps crossed with Connemara. Hunters are often three-quarters Thoroughbred or more; often the sire is an ex-steeplechaser on the National Light Horse Breeding Society premium scheme, formerly the HIS (Hunters' Improvement Society). They may have Welsh Cob, Irish Draught, Cleveland Bay or even some 'warmblood'. Again, certain sires seem more capable than others of producing the right type, given a suitable mare.

Riding horses do not yet have the predictability of type, nor even the predictable breeding, of riding ponies. They are often hacks that lack quality, or are undersized hunters, although no less useful for all that.

In the UK breeders still trail behind the rest of Europe in their ability to breed 'sports horses' except for eventers. Here Thoroughbred blood gives vital speed and scope, but many eventers have a drop of native blood, or even Arab, to give extra cunning and sure-footedness.

Whatever you hope to breed, go for a stallion with a proven track record as the sire of your ideal horse. Breeding pure is both easier and harder. Your choice of stallion is limited by the breed, but pedigree is very important and also adds a trap for the unwary. In-breeding and close line-breeding are for experts, so do not arrange any matings that look too closely related. If your mare is by a good stallion, try to find out if there are other mares by him, and which stallions have produced good results with them. This way, you can sometimes reproduce (or try to!) successful crosses of larger studs. Let the experts find out what lines 'nick' well together, then you can come along and copy them. Easy!

Some of us are colour-prejudiced about our horses. It is very difficult to make hard and fast rules, but there are two irrefutable ones: a chestnut mare to a chestnut stallion can only produce chestnut foals; to get a grey foal requires at least one parent to be grey. The colours of the ancestors beyond the immediate parents make no difference in this case. If you must have a grey, find a stallion who has *never* sired anything but greys and has also sired at least eight or so foals. Even this is not certain. He will probably also have turned white-grey quite early on, at two or three years old. Both his parents must be grey and we can hope he has inherited grey genes from them both. Grey is a dominant colour, and cannot be 'carried' unseen down the generations, hence the need for it to be inherited directly from a parent. Broken colour — piebald and skewbald — is usually like this too. If you absolutely must have a bay, your best bet is to put your mare to a stallion of a breed that only comes in bay, of which there is only one — the Cleveland Bay.

Well-kept mares and foals enjoying a stud's best asset; good grazing.

For most of us colour is just a bonus, but for palomino breeders it is a must, so a quick word on that. If you try to breed a palomino from a bay, brown or black mare, you are likely to get shades of dun instead. If your mare is grey, and your foal turns out palomino, sell it to someone who does not care what colour it is because it may actually be grey, in which case it will go white before long! Greys are never born grey but are born the colour they would have been if not grey (i.e. if grey was not the dominant colour), and then go grey with age. Chestnut mares to palomino stallions will have either chestnut or palomino foals. If both parents are palomino, then you can add cremello to the available colours. A cremello filly

born of palomino parents, put to a chestnut stallion, will always have palomino foals.

You can find details of stallions advertised in the equestrian press, in the *National Stallion Association's Directory*, in information from the breed societies and from their year books, magazines or stud directories. Go to as many shows and events as you can and if you see a horse that takes your fancy, do not be nervous about asking the owner how it was bred. It may take over a year to find the right stallion. When you want to see a horse, always make an appointment, and then always keep it or cancel in time, and ask to see the progeny as well. Tell the owner what you are hoping to achieve and if possible take some photographs of your mare to show what she looks like.

In the end you will find a nice stallion, with luck not too far away, at a price you can afford, and standing with people you trust. They should have good facilities and you should have no qualms about leaving your mare there. They should promise to keep you informed of what happens with your precious mare while she is in their care. You may be asked to fill in a booking form and perhaps leave a deposit. Deposits are a form of legal contract and are non-returnable under certain circumstances.

(*Above and left*) Healthy Arab mares and foals reflecting the good care their owners give them.

4. SENDING YOUR MARE TO STUD

You will have to decide what suits you as a good time for foaling when you are working out when to send your mare to the stallion. The average gestation period of a mare is 340 days (11 months and five days) but this is notoriously variable (three weeks either way is nothing!). If you plan on seeing the foal born, you will have many sleepless nights, which are not fun in March. The most natural time for foaling is May, but April foals will have the edge if you want to show. Earlier than that, I would leave it to the professionals who have grooms to sit up for hours on cold nights. An April foal will mean sending the mare to stud sometime in May.

Light, increasing day length and feed.

Mare comes into season.

Mare in season (oestrus); oestrogen produced by a follicle in the ovary.

6 Days

15 Days

Mare not in season (dioestrus); progesterone is produced by the yellow body in the ovary.

Ovulates on the day before going off.

Goes off.

Three-week oestrous cycle.

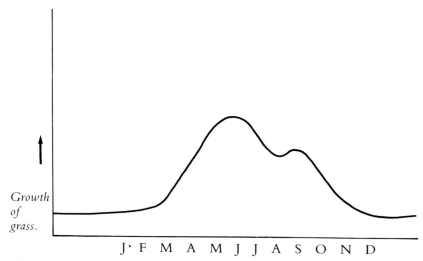

Growth
of
grass.

J F M A M J J A S O N D

The natural foaling time immediately precedes the maximum growth of grass.

From about March onwards, the mare should start to come into season. She will be in season for five to six days every three weeks, so she will be 'off' for around 15 days before 'coming in' again. This will be much easier to spot if she is turned out with a gelding. As she comes in, her temperament will change. She will be more ticklish, but may be more affectionate. You will notice a sticky discharge from the vulva, which will make her tail dirty. The vulva itself may lengthen, and will be much redder on the inside. When you brush her tail or sponge her dock, she may even 'show' to you, by lifting her tail and 'winking' at you. Mares also do this immediately after staling, but when in season the membranes look much moister and redder. Mares also stale more frequently when in season and will call to other horses more. Make a note in your diary of the days you think she could be in season.

The stud will probably require certain swabs, and a uterine lining swab should be taken when she is in season and the cervix is relaxed. Uterine swabs are essential. Most veterinary practices also take smears from the uterine lining to look for the presence of white blood cells which indicate infection. The cervix and vagina are not routinely swabbed as these may be contaminated by bacteria and bugs sucked in with air. Some mares do not show signs of being in season, but here the stud

(*Opposite, left and over*) Even obviously healthy foals such as these can deteriorate quickly; vigilant observation will spot potential trouble before it becomes a problem.

environment may help; the presence of other horses and especially the stallion may stimulate her to display normal oestrous behaviour. Other 'artificial' means of bringing a mare into season must be dealt with by a vet. For example, a vet can administer an injection which will bring the mare into season. This is not uncommon, and some mares may need a little help.

The vet may also take a clitoral swab, which can be done at any time. Cultures from these swabs will reveal the presence of harmful bacteria. Should the mare be infected with anything unpleasant, the vet will prescribe treatment to clear it up. He or she may well swab again to check that this has been effective.

In order to save you this expense, some studs will not ask for swabs to be tested if the mare has never been covered before (i.e. is a maiden) or has never had difficulties getting in foal or foaling. Most will insist on swabbing if the mare has been unsuccessfully covered (i.e. is barren — this confusing term does not mean she will never breed, only that she did not get in foal this time) or had a difficult foaling last time she bred. For your own peace of mind, however, it is best to have her swabbed.

Having all the necessary veterinary work done before the mare goes to stud saves time and expense, and also allows the stud to get on with the business of putting your mare in foal.

Arrange for the mare to go to the stud a few days before she is due to come into season. This will give her a chance to settle in her new surroundings before being covered. Travelling in-season mares very often makes them 'turn', so instead of having her covered straightaway, you are then faced with a three-week delay.

The mare should arrive at the stud in good condition, i.e. fit rather than fat. If she gains weight while she is there, it can help her to get in foal, but she should not start out by being poor. Try to avoid the need for rugs or any other equipment. Leave her with a well-fitting headcollar, preferably with her name on it, which can be left on her all the time. The stud owners may well add their own label or colour code to make sure they know who she is, and which stallion she is visiting. She should have had her hind shoes taken off and new front shoes put on if she is shod, or else her feet should have been recently trimmed. You should have wormed her a couple of days beforehand, and must remember to tell the stud owner when you did this and what brand of wormer you used. You will need to hand over her vaccination certificate, a photocopy of her registration document if she has one or it is not combined with the vaccination certificate, and her 'clean bill of health', resulting from the swab test. You should be able to assure the stud owner that she has not been in contact with any sick or infectious horses, confirm the date she is expected in season, remind them of any peculiarities she has, or extras you require, and finally let them know when you would like her back.

Most stud owners like to have six clear weeks after she was last covered, to make sure all is well. It is not reasonable to take her away as soon as she has been covered; that does not give the stud a fair chance to get her in foal and may invalidate any terms offered, such as NFFR (no foal free return) or NFNF (no foal no fee). If you are anxious to get her home as soon as possible, the stud owner may agree to her going home if she has not come into season three weeks after covering ('holds at three weeks'). Finally, check what times are convenient for telephoning and then leave your mare in their capable hands, trying not to worry too much!

5. WHAT WILL HAPPEN AT THE STUD

Visiting mares at stud are usually turned out together, those with foals being kept separate from maiden, barren or 'empty' mares (not covered last year). There is often a bit of rushing around when new mares arrive but this is natural and anyway none of them has hind shoes on, so the risk of injury is minimal. Each day the mares will be brought in for 'trying'. They are introduced to the stallion (or his frustrated assistant, the teaser, who does all the courting but none of the consumating) at a 'trying fence' which is a solid barrier that keeps the two apart, but is not so high that they cannot sniff and nibble each other over the top. The mare's reactions are observed and recorded.

Thoroughbred mare with twin colt and filly foals. Twins are extremely rare, normally being slipped (aborted) before they have any chance of survival. The mare wears a headcollar with an identity tag.

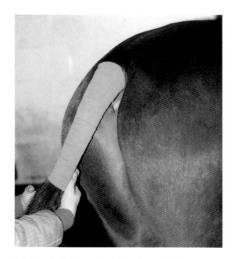

(*Above*) Mares' tails should be bandaged before trying or covering. A clean bandage is used each time.

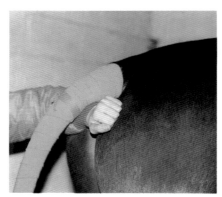

(*Above*) Reshape the tail following bandaging.

Mares that are ready will be covered, not on the first day they show interest, but usually on the third day they are fully in season and again on the fifth day if still in. The reason for this is that mares ovulate towards the end of their heat. Covering too soon is a waste of the stallion's energy and may upset or antagonise the mare. Missing out the fourth day does not reduce the chances of the mare 'taking' as most stallions' sperm will survive in the mare for at least 48 hours. However, if the stallion is not very busy, he may be allowed to cover your mare daily from the third day until she is going off.

Assisting at covering is a job for experienced people and it is not usual for studs to allow mares' owners to help or watch unless they know you well. The stallion is usually led by the same person who knows his routine and sticks to it. The person leading the mare will also be familiar with this routine and will make sure that the mare is under proper control and in the right place at the right time. An atmosphere of calm and competence at this time is essential. Emotions can run high all round; mares can be as evil, or even worse, than the stallions, so staff at well-run studs will take sensible safety precautions such as wearing a hard hat, carrying a whip and using a bridle rather than a headcollar. Seeing the stallion led out by a handler who is dressed protectively is not a slur on the stallion's temperament, but rather a sign that the stud is run safely and conscientiously. Your mare will benefit from these high standards.

Some studs run the stallions out with the mares. Usually the mare is covered 'in hand' first, as described above, then immediately turned out with the stallion. On some pony studs, this in-hand covering may be omitted but without it some stallions may well simply 'run' their mares, in other words, chase them! This is entirely natural, but if a mare has not been used to the natural way of life, she may be tempted to go through or over a fence. Such a system can be very rewarding — a good stallion out with a group of quality mares is a pleasure to see and the resulting foaling rates can be very high indeed. There is more risk of injury, however, especially if a jealous mare tries to guard the stallion and keep him for herself. This risk may be unacceptable if yours is a valuable show mare, but if you have the chance you may be prepared to take this

Stallion and mare are safely introduced either side of a solid trying board.

risk if you feel your mare would benefit from the natural method of breeding. It is important that the stallion is used to running with his mares, that the stud owner (or manager) is familiar with this system and that close observation is kept to enable fairly accurate records to be made of what mares the stallion is covering at any one time. The covering certificate should record the last date of covering (as usual) but a note should also be made of the dates the mare was running out, in case a later, successful but unobserved covering took place. Foaling dates more than five or six weeks away from the expected dates could result in the registration being queried.

At the other end of the scale is artificial insemination. This is increasingly popular with competition horses. One covering can be shared by around ten mares. It avoids the risk of infection being spread at covering, enables the stallion to inseminate many more mares and can result in higher conception rates, as it is all managed by a vet who will endeavour to inseminate the mare as close as possible to her ovulation, thus increasing the chances of conception. AI is not allowed by many breed societies, however, including the Arab Horse Society and the General Stud Book (Thoroughbreds). Check with your breed society if you are in doubt and want to use AI.

It is to be hoped that your mare will now be in foal. Her three-week oestrous cycle will stop. If she is tried again three weeks after she last came in season, she will be very standoffish with the stallion and she will now be said to have 'held at three weeks'. If trying (or teasing — same thing) is repeated with the same results six weeks after she last came into season, she is said to have 'held at six weeks'. For many people this is proof enough that she is in foal. The rest of us need more evidence!

6. PREGNANCY TESTING

The mare will be tried daily (or on alternate days) from around 14 days after she went off and for the next week. If by the nineteenth day or so she has not started 'showing', the stud may ask their vet to do a scan to confirm that she is foal. This is an ultrasound scan of the same type that is used on humans, but with a slight difference. The mare's embryo is too far away inside her large belly to pick it up from the outside, so the scan is done from the floor of the rectum, in other words internally. Most mares do not mind this. You may be given a print-out of the scan, which is an unusual and interesting 'baby's first photo'.

Naturally inquisitive foals often find cameras fascinating!

The scan can pick up the embryo from as early as 18 days from conception and will also detect twins. If twins have been conceived this is always bad news, and efforts should be taken to avoid allowing a mare to carry a twin pregnancy. The vet may advise starting again, or else at 24 days he may get rid of the smaller embryo by squeezing and bursting its sac.

There are many chances for a 'slip' twixt the cup and the lip and an early positive scan does not always mean that your mare will foal, therefore some vets advise a second scan at 42 days. It does mean, however, that the stud has successfully completed its end of the bargain. Not all vets or studs are equipped for scanning. A manual internal examination by the vet can confirm the pregnancy from around three weeks, so many studs use this method to confirm pregnancy in mares that have held at six weeks. Scanning is, however, more re-liable than manual palpation as the foal may have died, but the uterus not yet returned to the non-pregnant size. In any case,

(*Above*) Shahala (Arab) at the end of the summer. The grass is good and she looks well and in foal again, but this is just a grass belly.

(*Above*) Serenity (Anglo-Arab) at the end of the summer. This mare is also looking well and *is* in foal again.

you may not want your mare 'internalled', or she may object! Besides, not all vets make a common practice of it. In these instances blood testing can be useful. A sample of blood is taken from the jugular vein by the vet from 45−90 days after the last covering, in other words, at around two months. This is quite a reliable test but, as with any early test, a positive result does not always result in a live foal. It will not tell you if the mare has twins, and will remain positive during its valid time even if the mare has resorbed her pregnancy at any time after seven weeks. A further pregnancy test may be done to test for oestrone sulphate in the blood from 100 days onwards.

Even if you have been very cool and have accepted that the mare is in foal with no evidence other than her not coming into season again, you may later be filled with doubts as, in your impatience, you cannot wait for her belly to distend as final proof. From 150 days of pregnancy, a urine test is inexpensive if you avoid asking the vet to make a visit, but just hand the sample in at the surgery. It is as well to warn him that this is coming. He will need to know the identity of your mare and the date of her last covering.

Much patience is required to catch a urine sample. It helps if you know what triggers your mare to staling: the prospect of breakfast; a clean bed; the sound of running water and so on. Whistling to her may help. Putting your mare into another mare's stable may also help, but it should be a mare she is already in contact with to avoid cross-infection. Lurk discreetly in the stable armed with a clean bucket half full of clean straw to avoid noise and splashing. When she starts to stale, catch some in the bucket (250 ml is enough). It will be harder for her to stop suddenly if you let her start staling before you dive in with the bucket. Transfer the sample to a clean, screw-top jam jar for labelling and delivering to the vet.

When you get the result (positive!) you will also notice that the mare's shape has changed. Viewed from behind, the widest part of her belly is now much lower. At around four and a half months (this timing may vary), when it has become too large to remain within the pelvic area, the foal slips down into the abdomen. She may have a slight hollow in front of her hips. This distinctive change of shape may finally confirm her

condition for you. When viewed from behind, you may notice that the shape is not entirely symmetrical. The foal has to fit in among the mare's internal organs, in particular her caecum (part of the large intestine), which occupies a considerable proportion of the right side of her abdomen. As she walks away from you, you may notice that her belly swings from side to side in response to her movement. By the time she is ready to produce, the foal itself will weigh about one tenth of the mare's weight and the total weight of the foal, including the associated membranes and a lot of water, may equal one third of the mare's weight.

Tails in the sunset! Zorya's inflated shape can only be due to her advanced pregnancy.

7. CARE OF THE IN-FOAL MARE

Until the last three months of the pregnancy, your mare will not need any special care. If she was in work before being put in foal, then you can even carry on working her. Around three, six and nine weeks after covering, however, some people would suggest that the mare should avoid anything too vigorous or stressful. This is because she would come into season at these times if not in foal, and there is more risk of her losing the developing foal at these times. If you are not working the mare, then she will be best off being turned out for the summer. A lot is said about the risks of turning an in-foal mare out with geldings, but if she knows them, and was turned out with them before being covered, then the risk has got to be minimal, provided none of them is at all 'riggish'. It is better for her to be out with geldings than stabled all the time. If the grass is reasonable, the mare will need no supplementary feeding in the summer. Keep up the worming programme and other routines such as tooth rasping, farriery and vaccinations. The mare should keep good condition and may carry a bit of fat if not working, but she should not be allowed to become gross. Over the summer, ridden work may well continue as usual, but ease back on fast work and jumping. As you go into the autumn, the mare will start to get heavier and she may well give you hints that you ought to stop riding. You will find that the saddle may have a tendency to come forwards and make her more prone to getting galls under the girth as a result, so this must be watched. By the time the weather gets bad, around Christmas, you will probably both have had enough. If the mare is used in a riding

All horses need and enjoy company; in-foal mares are no exception. These three are content in each other's company.

(*Above*) This group of 'ladies-in-waiting' will sort out any differences they may have well before their foals are born, which will greatly reduce problems when they reunite after foaling.

school, the Riding Establishments Act forbids using in-foal mares during the last three months of gestation. This is a useful guide for all mares.

In the last three months, the foal is growing more and more rapidly. The mare will need extra protein and calcium to provide for this growth. She should have free access to good hay. A mixture hay or meadow hay contains a wide variety of nutritious herbs as well as grasses, and, if of good quality, clean and dust-free, may provide more minerals and be better than seed hay. Her extra feed requirements can be met by using a good make of proprietary nuts or coarse mix. If using nuts or coarse mix, do not go adding oats and barley, for instance, as this will upset the nutritional balance. Certainly never feed bran, as this can cause serious calcium problems. If you prefer 'straights' rather than mixtures, use hay or, ideally, lucerne chop instead of bran. Sugar beet is also an excellent 'filler', being high in calcium. Lucerne cubes or pellets (sold as alfalfa) are very good, being high in calcium and protein.

As the mare develops a bigger belly, it can be difficult to assess her condition. Get into the habit of feeling her neck,

(*Right*) This in-foal mare is in good condition; she has well-rounded quarters, and a good bloom on her winter coat.

back and the tops of the ribs, and viewing the hindquarters from behind. If she is losing body fat, keep this topped up with oats or barley if not feeding nuts or coarse mix, but always mixed with plenty of sugar beet and alfalfa for protein and extra calcium. As before, the mare must not get over fat.

By the last month, probably one third of the mare's diet will be hard feed, having gradually increased the amount over the previous two months. If you are using 'straights', these feeds could be half grain, half alfalfa by weight, with sugar beet pulp. Make all changes of diet gradually. Mares vary enormously; they are all individuals and need feeding accordingly. Some ponies need little more than hay, while certain Thoroughbreds could be eating as much as 6.3 kg (14 lb) of stud cubes a day (which is a lot of stud cubes!) as well as hay. it is important to respond quickly to her ever-changing needs.

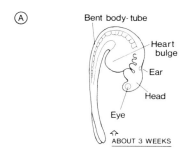

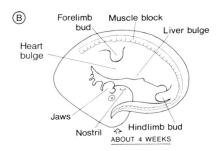

Suggested Feeding Guide for Mares

Type	Weight		Total feed	
	kg	(lb)	kg	(lb)
Arab	408	(900)	10	(22)
TB Hack	454	(1000)	11	(25)
TB Hunter	544	(1200)	14	(30)
Warmblood	590	(1300)	15	(32)
New Forest	318	(700)	8	(17)

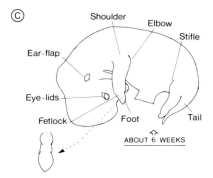

Daily Ration of Hard Feed (balance given as hay)

	Early preg. (light work)		1–3 mths before foaling		Last mth before and after foaling	
	kg	(lb)	kg	(lb)	kg	(lb)
Arab	1.8	(4)	2.75	(6)	3.5	(8)
TB Hack	2.25	(5)	3	(7)	4	(9)
TB Hunter	2.75	(6)	4	(9)	5	(11)
Warmblood	3	(7)	4.5	(10)	5.5	(12)
New Forest	0.9	(2)	4	(3)	2.25	(5)

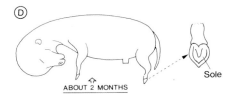

(*A–D above, E–G over*) Sequence of horse embryos and foetuses of increasing prenatal age. The ground or bearing surface of the foot is shown at 6 weeks, 2 months, 6 months and 9 months gestation.

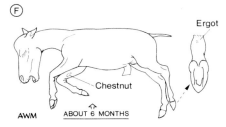

E

STANDARD LENGTH

x   x

ABOUT 4 MONTHS

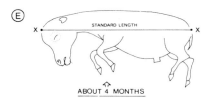

F

Ergot

Chestnut

AWM   ABOUT 6 MONTHS

G

Ergot

Frog

ABOUT 9 MONTHS

(*Below*) Foals learn from their dams.

However heavy and ungainly she becomes, your mare must have daily exercise. If you cannot get her out into a paddock, then walk her in hand. Two half-hour 'mooches' are better than one lasting an hour.

If she has been shod, then you will need to have all the shoes off before she foals to reduce the risk of injury should she tread on the foal. Do this two or three months before she is due, so that she can get used to having no shoes. Keep her feet well trimmed and if she has poor hooves, add seaweed (kelp) to the feed daily. *Do not exceed the recommended dosage.* If you are worried about your mare's feet discuss feed supplements with your vet and hoof management with your farrier.

Six weeks or so before foaling, the mare may start to show signs of 'bagging up'. The mammary glands increase in size and start secreting milk. At first this is a clear, straw-coloured fluid. You will notice that her 'bag' (udder) looks more swollen before exercise than after. The veins in this area also enlarge. At this time she may start getting filled legs. If possible increase the exercise time, but keep it gentle. Do not make further increases in the grain element of the feed if you can manage this without her 'dropping off' (losing weight). If you lead her out in hand, let her graze emerging herbs and weeds from the hedgerows and verges. Dandelion is a natural diuretic and she may well go for this. Should the problem continue, however, call the vet.

As the udder enlarges, it may get tender, especially if the mare has not foaled before. Gently rubbing in liberal amounts of baby oil will help to make it feel more comfortable and will also clean off any accumulations of dirt, grease and dead skin. Some mares resent this, so do not upset her by insisting on doing it. It is not worth the risk of being kicked or the mare getting distressed.

As D-Day approaches, the udder will remain full even after exercise. The muscles of the hindquarters will be soft and will wobble when tapped. Her tail will lose its tone. You will need to keep a close eye on her. If she is not already there, move her to her foaling box and check on her last thing every night. Give her a good deep bed, banked up at the sides and covering *all*

Koppélia (Arab) looking very heavy two days before foaling. The muscles on either side of her tail and croup are very soft.

the floor. Straw is best, shavings are not suitable; they can restrict a foal's breathing. Skip out and refill the water buckets (no handles on these to avoid the risk of injury) so that she gets used to you pottering about in the night. If you leave the stable light on (replace a high-watt bulb with a lower wattage), you will not disturb her as much as suddenly waking her up by switching on a blinding light.

Your 'foaling kit' should be ready by now. At the stable, you will have a skip, fork, barrow, head collar and rope and extra bedding. Get into the habit of wearing a watch if you do not usually do this, and carry a notebook and pencil in your pocket. The notebook will have useful numbers in it, such as the vet or an expert friend, and in this book you will note any changes in the mare's condition, together with the date and time. If the stable is miles from a telephone, consider buying (or borrowing) a portable cell telephone so that you can call the vet without delay if he or she is needed. Soap, towels and water for washing are a help. Be prepared to make a midnight feed for your newly foaled mare. Traditionally, this is a bran mash, but if you have given up bran, chop and sugar beet

Chriselda (Arab) sweating patchily on a warm evening in May just one hour before her foal was born.

with a few oats will be much enjoyed. A clean towel, well rinsed after washing to remove any detergent smells, should be available in case the foal needs rubbing down.

An emergency feeding kit will consist of a measuring jug, clean bottles (0.75 litre/$\frac{1}{2}$ pt beer bottles are quite good) and a couple of lamb's or calf's teats (from an agricultural supplier). A foal that needs hand feeding may not be totally healthy. If you do not have a proper foal rug, do not worry, an old *clean* sweater or cardigan will do instead. Also make sure you have salt and sugar in stock, and know where you can get replacement foaling milk powder. Some saddleries stock it or will order it for you; the Foaling Bank will supply all you need for orphaned or abandoned foals but there will be a short delay before this arrives, so it is best to be prepared yourself.

The nice bed provided for your mare will take a lot of mucking out. Do not ever be tempted to use deep litter or to do a quick and easy 'edges to middle'. It must be mucked out completely every day, with every inch of floor really well swept. You do not want to risk manky, germ-ridden bits being dug up by an anxious mare, ready to infect the foal with whatever is going. It is better to avoid infection in the first place by having good basic stable hygiene, rather than relying on treating the results of sloppiness with antibiotics.

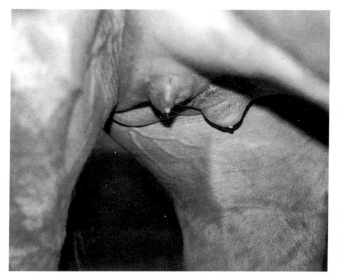 

Wherever possible, avoid planning on having two foalings in the same box in the same year. This increases the risk of infection enormously. If two foalings are unavoidable, then the bedding must be completely cleared out and destroyed, the box should be swept, steam-cleaned (or pressure-cleaned) twice and then disinfected and left to dry in the air for two weeks if possible. The woodwork should be recreosoted and the stone/brickwork repainted.

Ideally, your mare should be in her foaling box for at least six weeks before foaling. Each stable or yard has its own set of germs. In the six weeks before foaling, the mare has time to make antibodies against the pathogens in her environment and these will be passed to the foal in the first milk (colostrum). Also, she will be calmer and more relaxed in familiar surroundings.

(*Left*) Koppélia waxed-up the day before foaling. Some mares have much more wax, but many do not wax at all.

(*Right*) Filled legs can sometimes be a problem with heavily in-foal mares. Koppélia has filling along her belly which is also seen on occasions.

8. THE LAST COUNTDOWN

In the last couple of days before foaling, your mare may become very uncomfortable and restless. If she usually lies down in the night, she may stop doing this as she is now so heavy that it is becoming very difficult for her to lie down and get up again. Her appetite may drop and even if she eats her hard feed, she may eat less hay. Her bag will be full and remain so after exercise. The first secretions, which are clear and straw-coloured, may seep out through her teats and dry to form crystalline deposits resembling grains of brown sugar. In the last day or so, the milk takes on its more familiar colour, as its mineral content changes. In particular, its calcium level goes up. This change is easily detectable, and is the basis of a foaling prediction method. The milk now seeping out forms drip-shaped deposits, not unlike the wax that drips from a lit candle, hence the term 'waxing up' is used. Most mares wax up 24–48 hours before foaling; some wax up one or two weeks ahead and others are never seen to wax up at all. Even if you do not see the wax, you may notice damp streaks on the inside of the hocks and gaskin of the hind leg, where milk has dripped off and marked the mare's coat.

The mare's vulva also lengthens noticeably at this stage, and the whole perineal area becomes softer and flatter. The lips of the vulva may even gape. Your foal could arrive at any time now. Put a clean tail bandage on the mare and do not leave her for more than two hours. Ideally, stay with her, but be very quiet and discreet. Observe her but remain unobserved by her if possible.

In the last stages, she may 'run milk' from her teats. As she goes into the first stage of labour, jets of milk will squirt out more or less coincidentally with the contractions of labour.

(*Above*) Milk dripping from the teats, and splashes of milk can be seen on the inside of the hock. (*Below*) Smartie foaled two hours after this photograph was taken. Her vulva is long and gaping, everything looks and feels very soft, and she holds her tail to one side. The bandage helps to keep her tail clean and reduce the risk of infection during and following the birth.

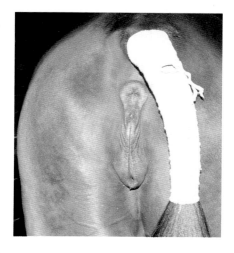

39

9. THE THREE STAGES OF LABOUR

FIRST STAGE

This stage starts with the first contraction of labour. The contractions increase in frequency and severity until the membranes rupture — the 'waters breaking' — at the end of this stage. While having contractions, the mare will experience colicky pains. Some mares sweat profusely, pace the box, glance at their belly and generally look and behave in an agitated manner. Very 'laid back' mares will pause momentarily in mid-mouthful, then carry on eating hay as if nothing is happening. Even if they do not sweat, most mares get a bit warmer and will feel slightly warmer or stickier to the touch. This phenomenon is made use of by foaling alarms, which are strapped round the mare's girth. The change of conductivity in the skin as it warms up in first-stage labour causes a radio signal to be sent to a receiver, which rings an alarm. All you need to do is remain within radio range.

If you want to see your foal born, do not leave the mare once she has warmed up. Her pulse and respiration will also have increased noticeably, having risen gradually over the last few weeks to a pulse rate of around 70, when she is close to foaling, as against the usual 40 or so. Avoid the temptation to interfere with the mare. Let her get on with it and keep your observation discreet. Make it an absolute rule not to have any non-essential people around. You may feel the need to have one other person for moral support — ideally someone who has helped to look after the mare lately, and whom she trusts. But *never* have extras ooh-ing and aah-ing on the sidelines.

(*Above*) Mare wearing foaling alarm.

(*Below*) Mares usually lie down at the start of the second stage of labour.

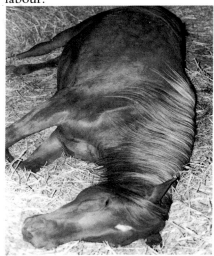

Ⓐ Parturition: intact package is squeezed by uterus to open birth canal; foetus upside down Ⓑ Parturition: outer membrane bursts: foetus is turning Ⓒ Parturition: amniotic bag swells out through vulva: foetus has turned and entered birth canal. The foal is drawn disproportionately small to show membranes clearly.

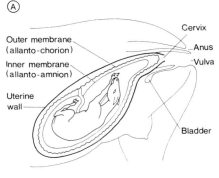

Ⓐ

Outer membrane (allanto-chorion)
Inner membrane (allanto-amnion)
Uterine wall
Cervix
Anus
Vulva
Bladder

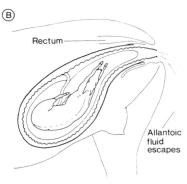

Ⓑ

Rectum
Allantoic fluid escapes

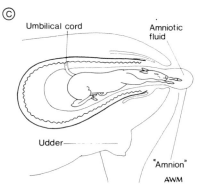

Ⓒ

Umbilical cord
Amniotic fluid
Udder
"Amnion"
AWM

During this stage, you may notice the foal moving around, apparently quite violently, in places you did not realise a foal could reach. This is normal. The mare may half lie down, even going onto her knees, then change her mind and get up again. Again, this may look odd, but is normal. Finally, the mare may groan and wobble for ages on her knees, then at last flop down — possibly her first lie-down for days. At this point, a whoosh of water — or even a small trickle — will announce the end of the first stage and the beginning of second-stage labour. Sometimes, the water goes while the mare is standing, and she may even remain standing, however most mares lie down. The water bursting is like uncontrollable staling and is usually the colour of weak, milkless tea. You will be amazed at the volume!

The length of time a mare is in first-stage labour is very variable and depends largely on your detection of it. Around one and a half hours is usual. If you are sure she is in labour and if it goes on longer than this, call the vet, especially if the mare is hot and distressed. While you are away making the call, she will probably have the foal!

SECOND STAGE

The second stage is the actual delivery of the foal. Make a note of the time the waters burst, because one's own sense of timing is not reliable on such a momentous occasion.

Most mares deliver lying down. Although the placenta has broken and allowed a lot of water to escape, the foal is usually still enclosed in the intact amnion. This membrane is a bit like a white plastic bin liner. The foal's front hooves should be the first part to appear, one slightly behind the other. The feet may look larger than you remember any foal's feet to be; this is because they are padded out with so-called 'golden hoof'. This is actually white not yellow, and is a fragile, almost jelly-like tissue which protects the mare from damage by the foal's hooves. It comes off when the foal stands up. The muzzle should appear next, lying on top of the forelegs. The soles of the feet should be facing towards the mare's hocks. The foal's head should lie on top of its forearms. Up to the muzzle's

(*Top*) The two forelegs arrive first, one ahead of the other; the leg with the white stocking is in advance of the other leg.

(*Centre*) The foal's muzzle has now appeared.

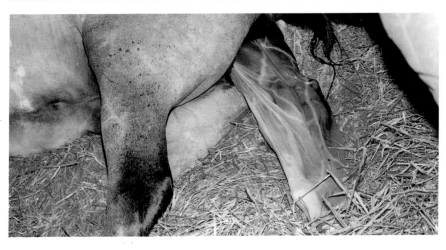

(*Bottom*) Here we see the head and neck extended along the forelegs. The almost transparent white amnion is still intact. The streamlined shape of the foal makes delivery relatively quick for horses compared to some other species.

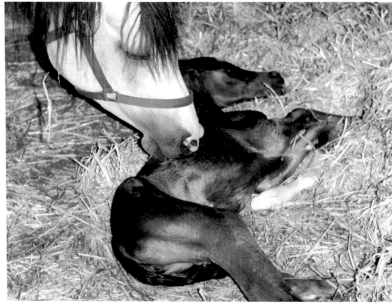

(*Above left*) Arab mare and pure-bred foal. Delivery is complete and the attendant makes sure the amnion is clear of the foal's head. The cord is still intact.

(*Above right*) Shortly after a successful delivery, the mare will lick, nuzzle and nip the foal to encourage him to get up.

(*Below*) Help is occasionally needed to complete delivery.

appearance, progress may have been very quick, but the foal's forehead creates extra width and so needs a good push from the mare. It is quite normal for the mare to get up and walk round at this stage. This can actually be beneficial, as it can help improve the position of a foal that has not come fully round into the correct alignment.

Once the shoulders are through the birth canal, the majority of the rest of the foal slips outs and you can make a note of the time of birth. If the foal is large and the mare is getting tired (or getting nowhere) you may need to help. Gently pull one foreleg at a time – the shoulders will not get through if they are square to the mare's pelvis. Pull only when the mare is pushing, and only in the direction the foal is being born. Once the foal's knees are through, this direction is more or less towards the mare's hocks, not straight out behind her.

This stage is usually over in ten or 15 minutes. You should call the vet at any time you feel your mare is suffering or if she has been in second-stage labour for more than half an hour.

Once the bulk of the foal is delivered, the hind legs may remain in the mare. Leave them there, as it encourages her to rest and avoids risking the cord breaking too soon. If the amnion

(*Top*) Although only a few minutes old the foal is alert, aware and sitting up.

(*Centre*) An hour and a half after birth the foal is dry and steady on his feet; the dam has a well-earned rest.

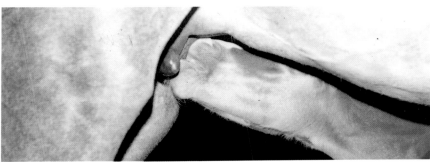

(*Bottom*) An hour later and the foal is suckling confidently.

(*Above*) The hippomane is a concentration of urinary salts between the placenta and amnion. Perhaps because of its rarity it was once considered lucky. The hippomane is, however, of no importance, and you should not be concerned by its presence.

is still over the foal's head, tear it away and wipe the mucus from its nostrils. Once the foal is completely out, I also like to smooth the mane onto the offside while it is still wet, in the personal belief (probably misguided) that it is then more likely to stay on that side as it grows! If the foal is lying out of the mare's reach, you could quietly pull it round to her head by dragging it by its front legs, so that she will not have to get up to tend it. My mares get a warm feed in bed (from a bowl or bucket without a handle) while the foal is busy discovering it is out and could think about getting up. It is best to keep a very low profile, providing all is going well.

THIRD STAGE

This stage begins with the safe delivery of the foal, and is concerned with the expulsion of the after-birth, known as 'cleansing'. It varies enormously from mare to mare. Some cleanse immediately, others take hours. They tend always to run true to their own established form, so make a note of the time taken this time, then you will not get any surprises next time.

(*Above*) The after-birth (placenta and other membranes) laid out for inspection.

(*Right*) Delivery of the after-birth follows the delivery of the foal. This mare is cleansing almost immediately; other mares may take several hours.

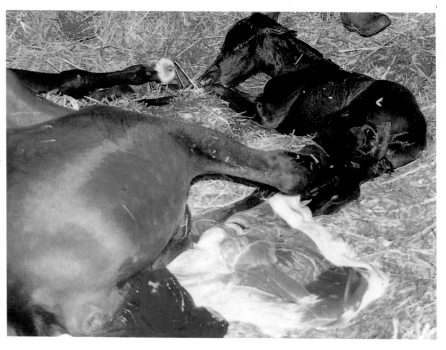

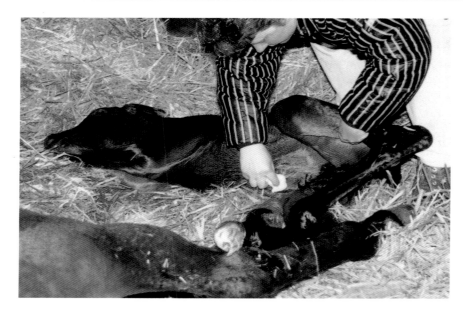

(*Left*) The stud groom applies surgical spirit to the umbilical stump.

(*Below*) Tying up the after-birth.

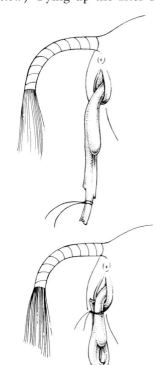

Once the mare has recovered from her efforts, she will get up and this is usually when the cord breaks. It is best to leave it intact as long as possible as the foal will go on getting blood from the placenta as long as there is a pulse in the umbilical cord. Once it has broken, which normally happens close to the foal's belly, leaving a couple of inches of stump, it should be dressed with antiseptic to reduce the risk of infection. Antibiotic spray (purple) is effective, or even a slosh of surgical spirit. The after-birth should be removed immediately and kept for inspection in a clean bucket and, if it can be achieved quickly and quietly, the worst of the wet straw should be exchanged for clean.

If the mare does not cleanse straightaway, the after-birth should be tied up with clean string to prevent her from treading on it and tearing it. Tie the string tightly round the end of the membranes, then loop them up and tie it tightly again, as high up as possible. If necessary, loop and tie again.

The foal will make many vain efforts to get to its feet before it finally makes it. The dam will help by nibbling, licking and pushing it. Most foals are up within one hour of birth. If it is not up and does not look like being so soon, by two hours old, then you may need to call the vet or help the foal yourself.

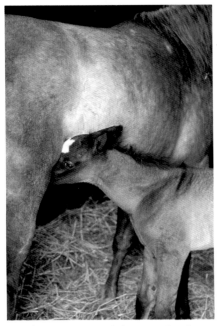

(*Above*) Zorya standing patiently while her first foal, Justinus, aged $2\frac{1}{2}$ hours makes rather inept attempts at suckling.

(*Opposite*) Standing up and learning to suckle is something that the foal should achieve by himself; avoid the temptation to help when it is not necessary. Shahala successfully helps her fourth foal through these important stages.

Once on its feet, it may wobble and fall, but each time it should get up quicker and should be making good progress towards suckling. The smell of the milk will attract the foal. It will also instinctively know to tuck its nose into a dark corner and will make mistakes before finding the correct one. The mare will help by keeping still and tipping her udder towards the foal by resting the opposite hindleg.

Throughout this whole process, your presence in the stable will cause confusion, so, if all seems well, it is best to go off and get a cup of tea while the mare and foal get to know each other. However, a first-time mare (maiden foaler) may be tired, frightened and generally uneasy about her unexpected visitor. If she is unduly fussy or nervous, or moves off every time the foal is about to feed, it may be necessary to hold her. A headcollar should be sufficient, or a bridle, but never anything stronger. A twitch could cause a rise in blood pressure which could trigger a fatal haemorrhage.

Position the mare with her rear-end to a corner, so that only the near side is available to the foal. Be very gentle and patient with her. Distract her with feed if that helps, or hold up her near foreleg. Do not get cross if she squeals or kicks. Patience usually wins, but if you have not seen the foal have a drink by the time it is three hours old and it does not seem likely that it will feed fairly soon, call your vet as you may have a problem. Unlike some species of animal, foals cannot wait until the morning. They need their first feed quickly and subsequent feeds frequently.

The first milk, the colostrum, serves several functions. It is laxative and helps the meconium (the first droppings) to be passed without difficulty. It also supplies the foal with antibodies. The foal is born without any immunity at all, and until it is old enough to start making its own (at around three months) it depends entirely on the immunity it receives from the mare's milk in the first 24 hours. The foal's suckling also helps the mare to cleanse, as the hormones that let the milk down also cause the uterus to contract and expel the after-birth. You will also notice later how much the mare pulls in her abdomen when she feeds the foal, which helps her figure to return to normal.

If all goes well, you will need to do no more than check the mare and foal frequently, but discreetly, until you have seen the foal stand, suck and lie down, the mare has cleansed and the foal has dunged. Meconium is black and sticky, so even if you do not see it passed, you can usually see the evidence of its passing on the foal's tail or rear-end.

Should the mare still not have cleansed six hours after foaling, call your vet because problems can develop if this matter is left unattended.

When she has cleansed, check that the after-birth is complete. The placenta usually turns inside out as it comes away, so you will see a silvery, shiny surface. The other side, which is like dark red velvet, is the side which formed a close union with the mare's uterus. A complete placenta has only one hole in it, where the foal exited. If there are any other tears or holes, a portion may still be in the mare and she will need prompt attention from the vet to prevent infection. It is advisable to call in the vet as soon as possible after the birth of the foal, even if everything seems to have gone according to plan. An experienced eye checking the foal and after-birth will put your mind at rest. If the after-birth has to be kept until the following day, put it in a clean bucket, keep it wet and place it out of reach of vermin and dogs.

When this third stage of labour is complete and all is well, you can take a well-earned rest and catch up on some lost sleep! The vast majority of foalings take place during the quietness of night, and your mare will probably make every effort to exclude you. Respect her need for solitude. Offer the maximum of supervision, but the minimum of intervention.

Smartie is the only expert! The foal is her sixth, but for new owners Sally and Sue Falconer, it is the first foal. After the photo call, mare and foal were left in peace.

10. PROBLEMS

The vast majority of mares produce healthy foals without any problems for mare or offspring. Occasionally, however, things do not go right. The important thing to remember with mares and foals is to act quickly — do *not* 'wait and see'. Your vet would rather be called out for nothing than be called out too late only to tend a potential corpse. When to call the vet depends very much on your judgement. The best rule is, if you are not happy, call in the expert. Your peace of mind is worth the expense.

Tactile hairs are vital for communication between mares and foals and should never be removed.

Call the vet if you feel at any stage that your mare is suffering unduly. Also call him or her out if any of the time scales mentioned above are extended. Call if the foal is in the wrong position, which is anything other than that described above. Get help if the mare is failing in her maternal duties.

The foal will need attention if it fails to behave in a normal way, as described above. Meconium retention will cause colic, and the foal will lie on its back. Scouring should always be treated, as should any odd behaviour or strange noises from the foal. Reduced feeding needs action. The best way to check feeding levels is to feel the mare's udder. Full and hard suggests the foal is due for a feed. If it wakes and fails to get up, stale and feed promptly, suspect that it could be ill. Foals are very light (about one tenth of the mare's weight) and should look very sound and move with dancing steps. Lameness or lethargy needs attention. Keep an eye on the navel; if it is not drying and healing, or looks swollen or infected, call the vet.

Although young creatures seem to have amazing powers of recovery, they can also fail fast. Nature does not mind losing the odd foal, as long as the species overall keeps going, but our foal is precious and needs prompt, effective care as soon as it is ill if it is to survive and be strong.

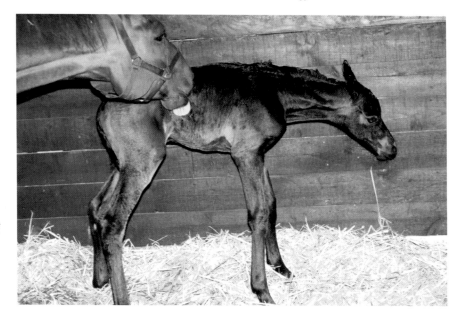

The foal's legs are still bent from her cramped prebirth existence but will straighten in the next couple of days. This happens occasionally with a large foal especially, as in this case, one born to a small mare. The mare is Anglo-Arab, the sire Hannoverian.

11. THE FOAL'S FIRST FOUR DAYS

This is the most critical time for the foal. Once over the first four days, you can relax (a bit)! If it is a nice day after the foaling, consider turning the mare and foal out. The ideal paddock is fairly small, sheltered and safely fenced. Barbed wire, netting or electric fences are best avoided. Lead Mum slowly and let the foal follow. Just 'field' or usher it along. Do not try actually to lead it yet. If it needs more help, put one arm round its chest and the other round its rump. Try not to support it or it will go limp and expect you to carry it. Take both mare and foal well into the paddock and make sure the foal is right under the mare's nose before you let them both go. Leave the mare's headcollar on and step back quickly without giving the foal a chance to follow you. Observe quietly from the fence. A couple of hours should be enough. This will allow you time to give the box a good muck-out and airing, and allow any dust to settle from bedding down. Make sure the bedding covers the whole floor, right up to the door, and is well banked.

Careful observation of the foal will reveal if all is well. It will feed frequently, hourly at least — some feed every half hour. After a rest it will get up, stretch, stale, feed, play, then rest again. It should be dunging easily and the droppings will soon turn mustard-yellow after the dark meconium has passed. Greedy foals pass more dung and it may be quite soft. The urine will be very watery looking and again should be passed with no problems or discomfort.

The mare may appreciate a quick but thorough grooming, but do not hang around gawping at the foal — she may resent this and even turn nasty. Any female who has just given birth

This Arab foal is enjoying a canter in a well-fenced sand arena.

During the first few days after the birth, the mare will be very attentive to her new foal not allowing him out of her sight. In these three photographs Shahala supervises new-born Ehriq's every move.

has every right to feel tetchy and temperamental and the instinct to guard the young baby is very strong. If you get seen off at this stage, it is not because she is vicious but because she is doing her duty as a dam.

Levels of feeding may need to go up. She will need plenty of high-calcium, high-protein food. Good grass is the best possible feed; if not available, give her more of the ration she was receiving before foaling. As before, aim to keep her in good but not fat condition. Try to arrange for the mare and the foal to be out as much as possible but avoid letting the foal get cold and especially being rained on. Late foals may also be bothered by flies on hot days, which will prevent them from thriving.

Between four and seven days, the foal and its dam should be able to start going out with other mares and foals if possible. It is not wise at this early stage to mix mares and foals with anything other than similar mares and foals.

Koppelia and Thomas enjoy their first outing together in a safely fenced paddock where they can be observed from the house.

12. REBREEDING THE MARE

Nature cannot afford to waste time in getting mares back into breeding condition after foaling. If they are to foal every spring, then they have to get in foal again within a month of the foal's birth.

The mare may start coming into season again when the foal is only four to six days old and may even be coverable when the foal is eight or nine days old. This is called the 'foal heat'. Most foals scour at this time ('foal heat scouring'). This condition in the foal may be due to hormones in the milk, or a greedy foal overfeeding, but it is more likely to be worms; infection with threadworm (*Strongyloides westerii*) is quite common in very young foals. It may also be due to natural changes in the young foal's gut development. If the foal develops any other symptoms, or becomes dehydrated, lacks energy or goes off milk, call out your friend the vet. Do not administer worming medicine to such a young foal unless under the vet's supervision.

Nine days after foaling, the mare may ovulate, so people who are keen to get her in foal rightaway will cover on this day. Around 40 per cent of such coverings (just one service) on the ninth day following foaling, will result in a foal, but the proportion of abortions and problem foals is higher than if covering takes place on subsequent heats. Many people regard nine days as too soon, so before taking this decision, consult the vet about any tests and examinations he advises. The main function of such an early heat is to cleanse the reproductive system after foaling. The secretions made by an in-season mare are an effective cleanser of many minor infections of the reproductive tract. However, this heat is very predictable, and

Do not feel pressurised into rebreeding your mare; take the time to enjoy your new foal.

Whatever their breed or type, all foals are enchanting.

some mares will then go anoestrus (fail to come in season again) after their foal heat.

The mare should return immediately to her three-week cycle (unless she is being abnormal), so the next season should start when the foal is 25 days old or so. The mare will be fertile on about the thirtieth day, or about one calendar month, after foaling. This is probably the best time to cover again. If the mare foaled late, the temptation is to use the foal heat to get her to foal earlier next year, but research has shown that your three-week advantage may, in fact, be only two weeks, as, in my experience, gestations following foal heat coverings are longer. The shortest gestations are those following covering at one month.

Foal-heat covering really necessitates foaling the mare at the stud she is booked in to visit, as travelling a very young foal is not to be recommended. If you are covering at a month, however, there should be no problem in travelling the mare and foal when the youngster is about three and a half weeks old, and the mare due to come into season. Travel them together in a double or treble compartment, or, if it is a small box or trailer, take out all the partitioning. Leave a headcollar on the mare, but otherwise travel them both loose. Make sure everything is safe, with nothing projecting that the foal could get hurt on, and no gaps etc. in which a hoof or leg could become trapped. There should be hay for the mare, but it is best to put it on the floor. Nets are not safe around youngsters as they can play with them and end up getting caught. Most foals lie down when travelling, so make sure there is plenty of bedding. If you are going a long way, stop every hour for ten or 15 minutes, to allow the foal to get up, have a leg stretch and a drink. Offer the mare some water each time as well.

Many mares breed happily year after year. Usually, if they need a rest, nature will see to it that they just do not get in foal. Just because she can breed, however, is no reason why you should. Only breed a foal if it is likely to be wanted. Do not breed again just because your mare is now a brood mare. If the mare is elderly (teenager or more) it is best not to breed every year. It is also wise to hold back if she had a bad time foaling, her condition has dropped off or if you had to feed her vast amounts to keep it on. If she has developed an infection as a result of foaling, a year out of breeding will give you and the vet a good chance to clear it. The alternative is covering and not getting a foal anyway, or large vet and stud bills and a late foal next year. Also, it is to be hoped that the foal she has is special to you and you may not want to miss a big chunk of its growing up while it is off with Mum at stud. Having the mare covered is, as you will know by now, only the start of a lot of time and expense, so only cover after thinking things over.

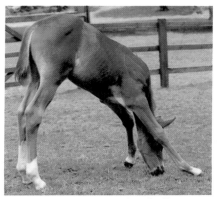

Learning to graze. The foal's neat and narrow jaws will grow to a proportionally large size to accommodate the large adult molars.

13. STABLE MANAGEMENT AND HANDLING

Young foals get into trouble just as easily as the young of any other species. The stable and paddock should be as safe as you can make them. In the stable automatic water bowls are preferable to buckets, because buckets are fun to play football with. If you have to have buckets, take off the handles and plant the buckets inside old tyres to help keep them upright. Fixed mangers are safer than hook-on portable mangers, which are easily removed and can cause injuries. However, built-in mangers should be boxed-in down to the floor to make them safe. Haynets are very dangerous to all young stock, who will chew them, undo the knots and play cats' cradles with them. Fixed racks, of a design to prevent seeds falling in the eyes, are better; solid-sided hay mangers at floor level are best. Failing these, feed the hay on the floor but be prepared for waste.

Have a good look round the stable. If there is a hole or gap big enough for a foal's foot, it will jam one in, so board up all gaps. It is vital that the door has a bottom bolt that you always use. Not only does it keep them in if they manage to get the top bolt undone, but should the foal lie down behind the door, it prevents the possibility of a foot being pushed through the bottom of the door and then getting stuck as the foal tries to get up. A top door that works is beneficial. Early born foals do not like blizzards blowing in on them and if you have to take Mum out on her own, you need to be able to shut the foal in securely. Electric lights should be in bulk-head fittings and any wiring in conduit and out of reach with a waterproof switch outside the stable and also out of reach.

Looking after horses is a year-round commitment.

61

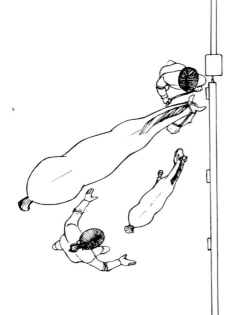

Bird's-eye view of the mare and handler forming a 'V' with the gate or safe fence. The foal can be quietly encouraged into the diminishing space where all escape routes are barred, and thus caught. All parties must remain calm and confident throughout the procedure.

Many proprietary demountable stables have insufficient ventilation, especially bearing in mind that you now have two inhabitants, not one. An alternative 'top door' cut in the wall opposite the main door can be used to provide a through current of air in very warm weather. Covered roof outlets will also provide extra ventilation.

The mare's manger or feed bowl should be large enough to allow the foal to share. From even one or two weeks of age, it will show an interest in Mum's food, even though it will be a month or so before it actually eats appreciable quantities. Personally, I do not think it necessary to give the foal any separate or additional feeding as long as you have good grass, the mare is feeding the foal well, and she will allow it to share some of her food.

The foal's education starts right from the beginning. However little it is, it must learn to give way to people — it must go back from the door to let you in, and must never be pushy. First halter lessons can start any time in the first couple of weeks, depending on your circumstances (having plenty of time) and the mare's behaviour (accepting your presence around the foal and tolerating you handling it). When you initially fit a foal slip (a special, small, foal headcollar), make sure that first of all the foal is in the corner of the box and cannot go backwards. Stand next to its body, put your right arm over its back, hold the foal slip in both hands below its head and quickly and quietly pop the nose band over its nose and do up the head strap. Talk to the foal all the time, keeping hold of it with your arms round its chest and quarters so that it does not run off. Find an itchy place and give it a little scratch so that the whole thing is a pleasant experience. Then let the foal go for a few minutes, while you watch, and then repeat the process to take the foal slip off. Do not try to hold the foal by the head yet.

When you lead the mare out to the field, the foal will naturally follow. Allow this to happen even though you will be going along, too. By the second or third day, rather than just guiding the foal to follow Mum, you can start leading it, but at first just with a scarf or stable bandage around the neck, and an arm round the hindquarters. To move the foal on,

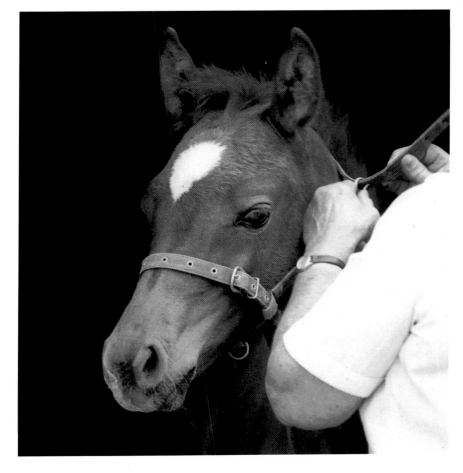

With patience and care your foal will come to accept his headcollar being put on and taken off.

push it from behind, never pull it by the neck. Each day practise putting the foal slip on and off. When the foal has accepted this, it can practise wearing it to go out to the paddock. Never leave it on while the foal is out, though. After a week or so of this, and if still leading by the scarf, switch to a soft rope. You will need one that is a bit longer than usual. Attach it to the foal slip, but use the rope as you did the scarf, without pulling on the head. Gradually, you can transfer to the headcollar direct, so that should the foal go forward too fast, you will check it on the headcollar. You will still need to push forward from behind, however, rather than pull on the headcollar. To do this could cause the foal to panic, pull back harder and fall over backwards.

(*Above*) A one-month-old foal being led from the headcollar. The handler sensibly takes the precaution of wearing a hard hat; foals, colt foals in particular, can be boisterous.

(*Below*) Horses are potential athletes and should be given the opportunity to gallop and play right from the start.

By the time it is a month old, the foal should be leading from the headcollar, and only need an arm behind for encouragement when it stops. By the time it is six or eight weeks old, you should be able to lead the foal in your right hand and Mum in the left. At first, you may need a helper to encourage the foal forward from behind if it stops.

Grooming can start almost by accident. The foal will become nosey when you are grooming Mum, and just to show it what is going on you can give it a stroke or two with the brush. The foal will soon enjoy this and start coming back for more. From very early days the foal should become used to having its legs handled and allow you to lift its feet — at first only just off the ground and for only a second. Gradually, it will let you hold them for longer and pick them out. If the foal tries to kick, hang on. If it ever kicks at you out of spite, slap it immediately, shout at it and try to arrange its routine so that it does not have the opportunity to kick you again.

All foals need to play, and if they do not have other foals to play with, they will try to do it with you. Never encourage this in any way at all. If you cannot arrange for it to play with other foals, arrange some other sort of company, such as a pony, which should be devoid of any hind shoes. Let the mare get to know the companion first, by turning them out in adjacent fields. There is usually no problem if you wait until the foal is about eight weeks old, and the companion pony is not pushy with your mare.

It is very important for the foal to have as much liberty as you can give it. By June, mother and foal can live out at night and will probably be happier coming in during the heat of the day, thus avoiding the flies. This will keep up the handling experience. If the foal is good to handle and has learnt to lead, it then does no harm to turn mare and foal right away for two or three months on good grass with other mares and foals. If the foal is checked and handled daily, even if it does not come in, it will not 'go wild'. Fields that have been cut for hay and then rested for a month or six weeks to recover, provide very good grazing for mares and foals, as they should be virtually worm-free. However, always worm both mare and foal before turning them out, even on 'clean' pasture.

Guide to Weights for Worming
Proportion of adult weight of a growing foal

Foal		Pony		Arab		Hunter	
		kg	(lb)	kg	(lb)	kg	(lb)
Newborn	1/10	27	(60)	41	(90)	54	(120)
6 months	2/5	109	(240)	163	(360)	218	(480)
Yearling	3/5	163	(360)	245	(540)	327	(720)
2 years	4/5	218	(480)	327	(720)	436	(960)
3 years	9/10	245	(540)	368	(810)	490	(1080)
4 years	(adult)	272	(600)	408	(900)	544	(1200)

The foal should be wormed from four weeks and monthly thereafter. The mare should be wormed at the same time. For the best results, use products that destroy migrating as well as adult worms. The first dose should be of a product that will kill threadworms, *Strongyloides westerii*. Young foals are very susceptible to worms and for that reason, if for no other, they should not be turned out with unwormed horses, or on pasture grazed in that season by unwormed or infrequently wormed horses. As far as is possible, mares and foals should always have 'clean' grass (not previously grazed that season by other horses).

Unless its feet are crooked or deformed, the foal's first trim will be when it is about three months old. Keep an eye on the feet after that, but it is unlikely that they will need doing again before another two or three months have passed.

When the foal is three months old it can also begin its vaccination programme. It will need 'flu and tetanus vaccinations at three and four months. Its first 'flu booster will then be when it is about ten months, and annually thereafter. In alternate years it will need a tetanus booster as well. The vet will fill in an identity document on which to record all the vaccinations. This is also an appropriate time to fill in the foal's registration papers, and send them off with the appropriate fees before the end of season rush!

The importance of equine company for horses of all ages, but for youngsters in particular, cannot be overemphasised.

Fresh air and freedom helps a horse to develop mentally and physically.

Companionship is important for youngsters. Part-bred Arab, Tammy, and Shetland, Bold Baron, are happy in each other's company.

They will thus receive a lot of discipline, not only from their dam, but from their companions as well. Every time a youngster is kicked or bitten, it learns respect; this is then a lesson you will not have to teach your youngster, and it is also likely that you will never receive such a threat from it. All horses are potentially dangerous just by virtue of their size. To allow them to feel they are 'top dog' and start using their size and strength against us is potentially lethal. If given equine companionship, when it comes to weaning our foal has babysitters on tap, whom it already knows, so when Mum disappears, it will not pine for long if it still has its friends. It will also learn to socialise, to understand horse language (it is, after all, a horse) and to be calm in the presence of other horses.

14. RESTARTING WORK FOR THE MARE

When the foal is becoming more independent and the intervals between its feeds are longer, it is reasonable to start working the mare again. The Riding Establishments Act says this cannot begin until the foal is three months old and this is a good guide for the rest of us. As she will be unfit, build up the work gradually until, after six weeks, she can manage an hour or so. Leave the foal in the stable with plenty of bedding, a small feed and the top door shut. Make sure it cannot try to escape — through a window for instance. There will be a lot of shouting at first, so take the mare out of earshot as quickly as possible. After a week or so, things will get much easier, as the foal soon realises that Mum always comes back. Watch out for your tack! Foals love chewing leather and can soon ruin a set of reins or even the saddle flaps.

Avoid strenuous work with the mare until the foal is at least six months old. She is already working hard feeding the youngster, and to give her strenuous, sweat-inducing work risks reducing the milk supply. If she proves nappy, having previously been willing, accept that you could be asking too much of her, and leave it another month or so. You will not be able to show or compete under saddle while she has a foal at foot. It would be grossly unfair to both, and in any case the mare cannot look or perform her best if she is feeding a foal as well.

15. WEANING

This is the complete and final separation of the dam from her suckling foal. It is often upsetting for both parties, but with tact and care this can be minimised. It is a very impressionable time for the foal and if not handled well it can result in an anxious youngster developing incurable stable vices, such as weaving and box walking.

Care should be taken over the timing. Usually, weaning should not be considered until the foal is at least six months old. If it is left until about seven and a half months, the foal's gut will have developed sufficiently to digest fibre, and the set-back of weaning will be much less, as the foal can now cope with a greater range of feedstuffs. So, for the foal, probably the later it is weaned the better, especially if it goes out every day (or is out all the time) with other horses as well as its dam.

The mare may have different ideas. Some 'earth mother' types will happily feed their foals to nine or ten months. If the mare is keeping condition and is not becoming bad tempered with the foal, then seriously consider weaning later than the traditional six months. If she is in foal again, however, it is important to get the foal weaned by the time it is nine months old, or when the mare is entering her last three months of pregnancy. Some mares become very surly with their foals, get fat themselves and limit the amount of suckling allowed to the point that the foal is dropping off (losing weight). Provided that you can arrange alternative company for the foal, this couple may be better going their separate ways when junior is around six months old. If the alternative is solitary confinement, however, then the foal is better off staying with Mum.

Kassya and Triple Time (both four months old) are confidently playing together, well away from their dams. Weaning will be less traumatic for these two if they remain together.

69

(*Above*) Two stables were knocked into one to make Serenity's foaling box. When it came to weaning, the large stable was partitioned into two so that the foal and dam could remain in each other's company while living separate lives.

(*Below*) Four-month-old Trincamalee with one-year-old Trisanna. Weaning will be no problem when youngsters have their older relatives for company.

Put them in a bigger box if possible, and feed the foal separately so that it demands less from its narky dam. By the time the foal is another couple of months older, it will be more ready to 'go solo'.

When the time comes, it is best to make weaning a clean break. The mare and foal should be separated and kept far enough apart so that they are out of sight and earshot of each other. If you have company for the foal at home, it may help if you send the mare away for a month or so. If they can hear each other calling, it will add very much to the trauma. If Mum is not there and cannot answer the foal's calls, it will soon resume its games with its companions and will quickly forget her.

Weaning in pairs often works well, so maybe you can arrange this. It is best if the youngsters already know each other and can share a large stable or a yard. It is as well to keep the top door shut for the first three or four days of weaning (if the youngsters come in) so that they cannot discover how to weave or be tempted to make a jump for freedom.

If you are lucky enough to have your mare and foal at a stud with others, they may all be out in a group, possibly with some yearlings as well. While the weather is kind, it can prove very successful weaning the foals one by one when they are turned out. Instead of turning the dam out with the foal, you let the foal go into the field where it will run off to play with its friends. Mum is then hastily removed, and by the time the foal notices that she has gone, it is a bit too late to worry.

Should you be in the position of having only the mare and foal, it may be sensible to take the foal to a stud for weaning. Take the mare and foal in the box, but drop off just the foal and drive off quickly with the mare. This is not the best method to choose, however, because the dam may get very distressed on her journey home. If you have made suitable arrangements, the stud will have another youngster of a similar age with which yours will go out. The excitement of new surroundings and new friends will soon make the youngster forget about Mum.

If weaning has taken place before seven and a half months, the foal will need extra protein, such as milk powder, and will not eat much hay. After seven and a half months, they manage well on a yearling diet. Unless you are breeding racehorses to go on the track at two years old, it is a mistake to stuff youngsters so that they grow fast and look fat. Slow growth is more likely to be appropriate. Upright feet and crooked legs are often the result of overfeeding. Young legs are not designed to carry a heavy body either. Of course, the youngster will need 'extras', but not supercharging! A good make of stud cube or coarse mix is suitable, or the same ration as the mare was getting when the foal was little − at least this will be familiar.

Once the youngster has settled after weaning, worm it again, with a product that will kill migrating worms.

Your young horse should be lively, keen to go out for exercise, play when it is out and be sensible to lead. Its coat should be glossy, even if it is as thick as a bear's. If you are feeding 'straights', balance the calcium with sugar beet and lucerne (alfalfa). The latter is also a good source of protein. Warmbloods and Thoroughbreds (and their crosses) seem to do well on oats, but ponies and Arabs may be bright enough already and be easier to handle if the grain balance is biased towards barley. Remember that barley is more nutritious than oats so feed by weight not volume; 1 kg (2 ¼ 1b) oats = 800 g (1 ¾ 1b) barley. Small native breeds may not need any grain at all, or very little. Alfalfa pellets are a good feed for these.

Cooked feeds are digested more quickly than grain that has merely been rolled, so you will need to divide such feed into three meals. Rolled oats and barley are digested more slowly and two feeds a day will suffice. As with all horses, routine is important and young stock will always do better if meal times are regular. If you decide to change feeds, do it little by little over a week. Of course, water should always be available. Towards the end of the winter your youngster (now a yearling) may be looking a bit jaded. Cod liver oil may help perk it up, and this or sunflower oil will also help its coat change. Most youngsters will need stabling at night through their first winter, but do make every effort to arrange as much liberty each day as possible. They will come to no harm when the ground is frozen, provided it did not get too poached before it froze solid. As for snow − they love it!

These youngsters form a happy, confident group away from their dams.

Mixed age groups are natural and the older horses help prevent the youngsters getting above themselves by teaching them manners and their place in the herd. For safety the older horses should not be wearing hind shoes.

The mare will also need special care at weaning time. Her milk supply must be dried up quickly so that she does not get mastitis. Also, if she has no milk to offer, her yearning for her lost foal will diminish. Her diet must be reduced immediately to hay and water. Twice a day for three days, she could have mash with 28–57 g (1–2 oz) (depending on her size) of Epsom salts. This can be a bran mash, but if you have given up bran, soaked sugar beet works just as well. Give her plenty of exercise, riding her if possible, or turn her out as much as you can. Do not milk her — the more you remove the more she will make, which is not the object of the exercise. Once the milk is going, gradually get her back on to a diet that is appropriate to what she is doing.

16. CASTRATION

The vast majority of colts will need castrating (gelding or 'cutting'). As long as there are two testicles in the scrotum, castration can be done at any age. It is said, however, that geldings recover quicker if they are cut before weaning — when they come round from the anaesthetic they can have a drink from Mum and will immediately feel better. On the other hand, if there are complications, a young foal will decline more rapidly than one a little older. A further consideration (apart from two testicles) is the weather, because if there are flies around, infection is likely, and if it is cold and wet, the youngster may get pneumonia. If he is kept in, he will probably swell up a lot. The best time to cut is probably April or May in fine weather before the flies are bad. The youngster will be coming up to one year old, should be reasonably well handled and not yet have become a problem with the fillies!

Castration prevents unwanted pregnancies and makes the horse infinitely easier to handle and much safer. He can live a pleasant life style, turned out in mixed company without worry. He will also grow more. It is not unreasonable to expect at least 2.5 cm (1 in) of extra height, and some people maintain that gelding at just the 'right' time (not disclosed!) can give another hand. Do not be sentimental about 'robbing him of his masculinity', just get on with calling the vet and go ahead with the operation.

Many vets will perform the castration on your premises. You may need to starve the youngster for 24 hours — check this with your vet. You will need a quiet, sheltered spot, preferably grassy and free from droppings. The lawn perhaps?

Although appealing at this age, colts quickly become a handful and will need castrating unless required for breeding when they will need expert handling.

73

Other vets prefer to perform castrations at their own premises, in which case you will need to make transport arrangements and confirm how long the youngster will stay there after the operation. If your vet prefers, he or she may cut your colt under sedation and local anaesthetic while the animal is still standing. This eliminates the need for the starvation required before a general anaesthetic. If the colt is castrated in a box, there should be a deep layer of clean straw on the floor. Gelded animals should not be bedded on shavings until the wound has healed because the shavings can enter the wound and cause complications.

After the operation the youngster will be very sore and dozy. Gentle walking in hand for half an hour will help. If he has to return to his box, close the top door so that he cannot doze off with his head over the door and throttle himself. A small, safe paddock, where you can keep an eye on him, is best. Some swelling is inevitable – he has had major surgery, after all, even if it is a routine operation. If, however, he is very uncomfortable, bleeding or discharging, you will need to call the vet back.

Familiar company helps castrated colts to recover more quickly.

17. FROM ONE TO THREE YEARS

Space and company are the best things you can provide for your young horse. If it can be turned away for the summer, nothing is healthier. If the terrain is varied, so much the better. Banks to scramble and hills to gallop up and down will help to develop natural balance and good bones and muscles. From the age of 18 months, you can stretch the interval between worm doses to six weeks, provided the pasture gets rested from time to time and the other horses sharing it are wormed at the same time. The feet will need trimming every two or three months. Enlist a reliable and sympathetic farrier, who will be firm without being brutish. In the meantime, make his job easier by regularly handling the youngster's feet yourself.

When leading in and out of the field, insist on good manners. Avoid leaving one youngster on its own, either in the field or in the stables. Always make the youngsters step back from the door or gate to let you in. When letting a youngster go in the field, always face the gate and make it wait until you are ready to let it go. *Never* hustle or chase it. Encourage it to come when you call at coming-in time — do not let it make you walk all the way up the field and then back again when it eventually decides to run to the gate. A few nuts will help to encourage good behaviour, but make this bribery less and less frequent, until the youngster comes out of good nature rather than greed.

If you get into trouble and cannot manage your youngster, seek professional help straightaway. Do not suffer fear or intimidation from any young horse; it is not worth it. Often, a short stay on a big stud where the staff have had lots of

(*Above and below*) Happy, healthy, well-grown, grass-kept yearlings.

Thomas is now rising three and enjoying the spring sunshine with other young horses.

experience with young stock, and where there are good facilities, will soon sort out a difficult youngster.

On good grass in the summer, the young horse should not need extra feeding, but once the weather gets chilly or wet, it will need to come in daily for a feed. As it gets older, it will need less protein, so you must gradually adjust the diet. By the end of the second summer (at 18 months old) the young horse will have finished most of its growing. It will slowly add another 5—7.5 cm (2—3 in) of height over the next two or three years, and gradually start to fill out. It will also start to become better looking again. Most youngsters 'go off' at six or seven months, and it will be another year before you begin to see the promise you thought was there as a little foal. The jawline of two to four year olds may look heavy and undulating. This is due to the development of the molars, which fill the jaw almost to bursting point. Remember, the jaw is likely to be very tender while the youngster is teething, so be sympathetic and make sure the headcollar does not rub. Some colts and show horses have to suffer chains under the jaw, which must be agony and not helpful in encouraging compliance.

It is unusual for young horses to grow evenly. Mostly, they grow upwards behind before the forehand eventually catches up. When they are 'up behind' they will look ungainly, the action will be less extravagant and they will not track up as well from behind. The shoulder may look straight, and the neck 'upside down'. In a few months, they will level up, but then the process may again be repeated. This is absolutely normal and is just a part of how horses develop.

So long as they have plenty of food and shelter, horses not yet in work can survive surprisingly harsh conditions.

18. SHOWING

Showing mares and foals can be great fun and very rewarding. It is important to pick the right classes, and to limit the number of shows attended. Look for 'mare with foal at foot' in the schedules. Sometimes classes are open to mares who have been covered in the current season as well, in which case you may need to produce your certificate.

It is not fair to show foals under four weeks of age, and in fact most shows make it a condition of entry that the foal is four weeks or over.

Foals under three months of age do not need to be vaccinated so long as the dam's vaccination certificate is in order. Over three months, they will need their own certificate. Herein lies a small problem. They cannot be shown until they have had their primary and secondary injections, which must be given at least 21 days apart (and not more than 90) and, additionally, ten days must have lapsed since the second injection. This means that you will have to miss a good month of shows. Of course, many smaller shows do not require stock to be vaccinated and even some larger ones recommend it but do not insist. However, it is as well to protect your foal if you are going to expose it to a lot of other horses at shows, so even if you do not have to vaccinate, you may decide it is a wise move. Regardless of rules, it is best to keep the foal at home anyway for the ten days following vaccination, as it will be more vulnerable to infection while its system is busy making 'flu antibodies.

The mare and foal are shown together, but if the foal will stand quietly in the line while Mum does her trot out, and vice versa, it can create a better impression and is easier for

(*Above*) Whilst showing is pleasurable and educational for the young horse, efforts to win should not compromise the foal's best interests. Clipping, even partial clipping, is not essential, although it removes the distraction of a faded, woolly coat.

(*Opposite*) A prizewinner. As the jaw develops, the distinctive domed forehead of young foals gradually disappears as the foal matures because the rest of the skull develops proportionally more than the cranium.

the judge. Practise this at home; if either party gets at all anxious, do not continue and do not do it at the show. Unhappy foals yelling for their dams, or even falling over, is distressing for all concerned and can be very upsetting for members of the public watching the class.

Both mare and foal should be groomed every day, but other than that their routine will not alter too much. The tendency to produce show horses that are very fat is, thankfully, declining, so do not go overboard in trying to get the mare into so-called 'show condition'. She should be well covered, looking fit and well, but not overfat. If the weather is unsettled, keep the pair in at night, and certainly keep them in for two or three nights before the show. Your mare may look better for a bath, but it is as well to avoid letting the foal get wet. If it is a miserable day at the show and you have shampooed all the grease out of its coat, it could get chilled and end up with a cold. Tactful use of coat polish, which most saddlers sell, will give the coat a sleek and shiny appearance, while the protective layer of grease still remains underneath.

A certain amount of thought needs to go into the equipment you will need. Native breeds and Arabs have their own traditions about show bridles or halters, and the mare should wear whatever is currently in vogue. If you do not want to buy anything special or expensive, a good leather headcollar, with the brass buckles polished, will look fine, or else use a snaffle bridle. Hack, hunter and riding horse types look nice in a double bridle. Of course, it is not the bridle that is being judged, but the horse, however, a clean, neat and appropriate bridle does create a good impression. Make sure that whatever you use will be sufficient to control the mare during the excitement of the show, and that nothing will break. Lead her with the bridle's reins, or a leather lead rein. A white web lead rein can also be used.

The foal will look best in a neat, fine, leather headcollar. Some native breeds go for white halters. Again, if you do not want to spend a fortune on new gear that the foal will grow out of in a month's time, you could use its usual headcollar or foal slip, but coloured nylon does not look smart and you could end up feeling embarrassed! The nylon headcollars sold

Heavy breeds and some native breeds are traditionally shown in white halters.

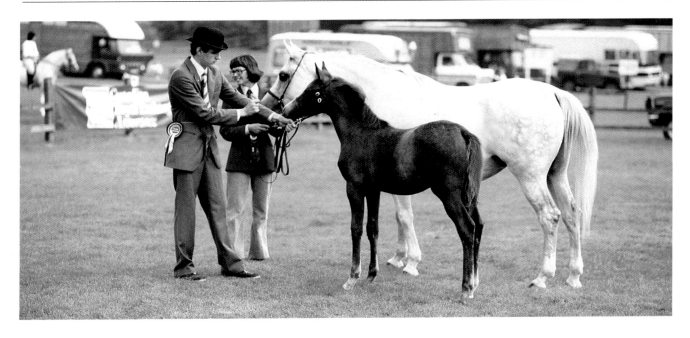

This Arab mare and her foal look neat and smart in fine leather.

for foals are very adjustable and very useful, so if you want to show, buy a good quality one in brown with brass buckles and then no one's sensibilities will be offended.

Foals can become very excited at shows, so it is best to use a rope rather than a lead rein, as you will get more grip on it. White looks smart; brown will do too. You will also find a longer rope useful — 3—3.5 m (10—12 ft) will enable you to hang on should the foal go up, whip round or charge off. You may need to ask a sailing friend to splice a trigger hook on one end of some suitable rope (from a yacht chandler) and back-splice the other end to stop it fraying. The effort will be worth it. Travelling has been outlined on page 59 and will be much the same for showing.

Native breeds and pure Arabs are easy to prepare for shows as they do not need to be plaited. Riding ponies or horses, hacks, hunters and the rest all need plaiting. If you intend to keep the mare and foal out as much as possible when they are not being shown, it may be better not to pull the mare's tail, but to plait it instead. Her mane, too, will need to be plaited, and so will have to be pulled a bit, but keep as much as you possibly can. Her foal will also look better for plaiting,

(*Right*) An impressive line-up of hunter foals.

(*Below*) Some breeds require a more elaborate turnout!

especially if it has grown a decent mane. You will not be penalised for not plaiting the foal, but it will certainly catch the judge's eye more if you have succeeded in plaiting it neatly. If the foal's tail will not plait tidily, it is better left.

In her carefree days before breeding, you may have been able to plait your mare the night before a show. Those days are over − now the foal will chew the plaits out − so you will have to get up early and may even have to leave someone guarding the plaits from the foal's inquisitive lips and teeth.

Once at the show, check your numbers, times of classes and rings. Allow plenty of time so that no one gets flustered.

Usually, the mares are judged first. They are led round the ring, on the right rein, with the foals being led behind their dams, or tucked in on their near side. The judge will ask the steward to call them into a preliminary line up. Give a little more space than usual, to avoid upsetting the other mares or risking the foals being kicked. The foals should ideally be held behind the mares. The mares will come out one at a time to be judged. As in other in-hand classes, it is usual to stand the mare up in front of the judge, then to walk away, trot back, round the ring and retake your position in line. If the foal will not stand quietly, it can be led behind the dam at a discreet distance, or alongside, but keeping it on the side away from the judge, so as not to cause any distraction or obscure his view. After judging, everyone usually walks round again before being finally lined up for the presentation of awards. Then it is the foals' turn. They will now all be brought forward to stand in front of their dams for judging. For the walk and trot they can be accompanied by the dam, but this time, of course, keeping the foals on the judge's side of the mare. At some larger shows the foals are judged quite separately, even by a different judge in another ring.

Should you be lucky enough to be well placed, check up on any further commitments, such as a parade of prizewinners or a championship. Failure to attend these can result in disqualification or at least forfeiting the prize money. Avoid hanging around the rings waiting for classes, but return to the box so that the foal can have a drink and a rest. The mare, too, may appreciate some water, a small feed and hay to nibble during the wait. It is always unfortunate if your class runs straight into the championship, as the mare and foal may by now be tired but will have no chance to recuperate.

Remember the judges' decision is always final, so do not be tempted to argue with them. Really, if you think your foal is wonderful, it does not matter what anyone else thinks! In any case, the most important judge (after yourself) is the audience watching. Many disappointed exhibitors, well out of the ribbons, have been pleasantly surprised to be approached after the class by a total stranger who spotted potential the judge has missed. Some will even make you an offer for the foal.

All foals are woolly, but some more than others. Not everyone approves of the practice of some heavy-horse breeders who shave the dock.

19. PADDOCK MANAGEMENT

A paddock provides food, exercise and the opportunity to socialise. On very small areas, the feed value may become nothing if all the grass is killed by poaching. About 0·6 hectares (1½ acres) per horse, carefully managed on reasonable soil, however, can provide grazing and even hay.

Rather than ruin all the grazing by poaching the ground in the winter when it is wet, it is best to keep the horses off it once it gets waterlogged and is cutting up. To avoid losing the benefits of fresh air and exercise, a small section can be fenced off as a sacrificed area for winter use. This may be more satisfactory if it has an all-weather surface (which is expensive) or a very small area may be concreted and used as a corral.

The main areas of land need dividing into three paddocks. One can be closed up for hay. If you are sure your stable muck is well rotted to ensure worm eggs have been destroyed, this can be spread on your hay field over the preceding autumn and/or winter. If you can swap your manure for a local farmer's cow muck, you will have a good fertiliser with no fear of worm infestation. The other two paddocks can be grazed once the ground has dried out enough. Alternate between the two, grazing each for three or four weeks while the other rests. As soon as the horses are off, harrow the paddock to spread the droppings so that the sun can dry them out. This kills worms, and allows the muck to be absorbed into the soil as fertiliser. It also helps to prevent patches of rough grass developing at the expense of over-grazed lawns. By the time these two paddocks are looking a bit worn out, the hay field will have had three or four weeks' rest since it was mown, and will be ready to join the cycle. Next year, it will be the turn of one of the other paddocks to grow the hay.

Well-rested grazing is best for mares and foals.

Sound fencing is essential with young horses.

If rough areas of docks, nettles or thistles develop, slash these down (or 'top' them with a tractor mower) before the horses move on. Horses relish the wilted remains of these weeds, which they do not like when fresh. (Make sure that all ragwort has been pulled up and removed from the field beforehand because this becomes palatable, and very poisonous, when wilted.) If there are lots of weeds, cut them in two or three goes over a week or so, to prevent the horses stuffing themselves.

Using cattle or sheep to eat what the horses leave is good paddock management, but remember that more stock need more acres and also more housing in the winter.

Worming can be done to coincide with paddock changing, so that you are putting relatively worm-free horses onto relatively worm-free grazing.

If you are not able to rest the grazing for at least three weeks after harrowing, you may increase the risk of worms. Three weeks is considered a suitable time, because by then most of the worm larvae that hatched from the eggs will have died. Certainly you must not graze newly harrowed, unrested grass; the risk of the horses picking up a large worm burden is too high.

The use of fertiliser for horse paddocks raises many questions. Rich grass can cause that very painful disease of the feet, laminitis. The current feeling is that artificial fertilisers are best avoided as they tend to increase the spring 'flush' which is risky enough already. What is needed is a fertiliser that is slow-releasing and so will extend the growing season and also level out the surge of growth in May and June. Well-rotted stable muck is not as good as the farmyard variety, but at least it is helping to return some of what has been taken out. Seaweed products are also very good.

Grazing animals in general, and horses in particular, are notorious for making pasture sour or acidic. Applications of a liming agent are needed to counteract this. Agricultural lime can be used, or calcified seaweed, which is actually a form of coral. The latter product offers more minerals than straight lime and seems to encourage grasses and herbs to root more deeply. It can be spread by hand, too, which is useful on small areas.

(*Above*) Soon the nettles and docks will need to be topped, and the horses will have to move to fresh grass.

(*Below*) This paddock will need harrowing and resting soon to allow regrowth for summer grazing.

Reseeding small areas is easily done by hand, broadcasting a mixture of seed and soil. Use a seed mix specially formulated for horse paddocks. Ask the advice of a good agricultural seed merchant or saddler when choosing a branded product.

Good grass is the finest asset you can have for yielding a good return on your investment, in the form of healthy stock. If the grazing is good, your mare and foal may well not need any other feed at all as what they are eating will be balanced, healthy and natural. Nothing produces better milk either.

Good grass produces good milk.

20. MARKETING

It may be that you wish to, or have to, sell the youngster you have bred. If you take time and care over this, you will give yourself the best chance of finding the right home for the foal and also the best price.

Many breed societies hold annual sales of registered stock. The owner of your youngster's sire should be able to offer practical advice about the specific features of that particular sale, or you can send off for information from the breed society concerned. If you have the chance, visit the sale (leaving your cheque book at home, to avoid temptation) to see the procedure for yourself. Purchasers at such sales are usually looking specifically for your type of horse, so they are not as risky as purchasers at general sales. It is always best at any sale to remember that a very high proportion of horses sold at auction end up on a butcher's hook. Your horse should be very well prepared and presented, with a reasonable reserve. The horse should look every bit as good as if it were being shown at county level. It should be leading quietly and well, striding out freely. A colt is best bitted and led from the bit from two years old onwards. He should create the impression of being uncomplicated and ready to do whatever his new owner wants. An out-of-condition, unhandled and nervous-looking youngster does not create confidence in potential purchasers. Make sure all the paperwork is in order — registrations, vaccination certificate, freeze-brand certificate and any other paperwork there might be. Get the youngster's feet trimmed a couple of weeks before the sale. Youngsters should not need shoes, but can be a tiny bit footsore straight after a trim.

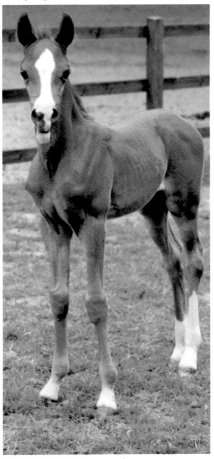

Encourage good manners from an early age!

Horses with extravagant action, such as this young Hackney, may present themselves better when shown loose in a paddock or field.

If the thought of public auction is too awesome, try advertising in the equestrian press. *Horse and Hound* is the main nationwide UK publication for hunters and riding horses, but you could try your local press too. An advertisement should be absolutely truthful and at the same time present your horse in the best possible light. If in doubt, stick to the facts of its expected mature height, sex, colour, breed, sire, dam and expected potential. It is better to say 'open to vet' than to state that it is sound. Terms such as 'bomb proof' cannot be substantiated and so are best not used. When you start receiving replies, do not be tempted to sell to the first person who contacts you, but take a few details about the home they are offering, and promise to ring back to arrange an appointment to view the horse. This way, you can to some extent choose your youngster's new home. Prospective purchasers who are unlucky should always be 'phoned back as a courtesy, explaining that someone who rang earlier than they did has bought the horse. Word of mouth can be effective but can take a long

time. Always tell the sire's owner if you are selling, as they will often have people contacting them who want a youngster by that stallion. Many of the breed societies have sales lists on which you can put your horse for a modest fee.

There is an increasing number of agencies which offer to find vendors and purchasers for horses. Some are computerised. These can be very successful if you have a horse in a popular category at a reasonable price. Commission is usually required from the vendor (you); it is as well to check beforehand how much this is and whether VAT will be added.

Once your horse has been sold, tell everyone who enquired that it has gone. You will want to keep in touch with the new owner, which is a good thing, but do avoid the temptation to pester them. A card at Christmas will probably yield an 'annual report'. Once sold, the horse is their, not your, responsibility.

Potential purchasers making preliminary viewings will often like to see youngsters in their natural state at grass, even before weaning.

The whole business of selling will be successful and easy if the initial advice was taken — breeding from a good, sound mare covered by a good stallion. Purchasers may ask what the youngster's dam achieved. Never be in the position of having to confess 'Nothing, she was lame'. Would you buy her progeny?

When people make appointments to see your horse, always allow plenty of time. They may misjudge the journey and arrive early or late. They may talk for hours and want to see every photograph you own. Regrettably, many will let you down and fail to turn up at all. Some will have you trot the horse up a dozen times, inspect every hair on its body, then ring two days later and tell you they don't like chestnuts. These are the time-wasters whom everyone involved in selling horses will tell you about. Apparently, estate agents have the same trouble with houses. They reckon on having 'sold' a house five times before they get a genuine purchaser, and it is about the same with horses.

When a prospective purchaser is expected, make sure the horse is in and groomed well with its hooves oiled. It is not necessary to plait up, unless the horse has a very unruly mane which looks awful loose but good in plaits! Use a smart leather headcollar and know where you can trot the horse up properly. Practise beforehand so that you know it will not spook. Allow the prospective purchaser to lead the horse about and put it back in the stable when everything has been done that needs to be done. Offer tea or coffee, then a last look before they go home.

Young foals sleep a lot, but not for lengthy periods. Try not to disturb the foal, you will not have long to wait.

21. CONCLUSION AND ACKNOWLEDGEMENTS

I hope that pony owners will forgive my use of the term 'horse' throughout this text. Wherever I use the word I am actually referring to all equines — horses, ponies, even donkeys. Breeding can be very rewarding in all ways (but not usually financially) and if this book has succeeded in giving you positive encouragement, then I have achieved my aim. The horse world is generally very friendly and helpful, so if you are new to breeding, do seek help. Your vet, breed society and the stallion's owner will, I am sure, all be allies in your venture.

Finally, I would like to acknowledge all the help and advice I have had in preparing this book: from my sister Fliss for ideas, editing and correcting proofs; Tony Hyett for comfort when it went wrong; Vicki Barrett for typing; my parents for starting the whole thing; my beautiful Arab horses for their inspiration and patience; staff and trainees at Heron Stream Stud; Jim Lees for imparting his knowledge; Caroline Burt and Jane Lake for encouragement; the livery owners at Heron Stream, especially Julie; friends at the AHS; Margaret and Sue Pelling; Mary Lloyd; and all those who allowed me to photograph their horses or who supplied photographs, especially my father, David van Lennep, and Bob Langrish, Stuart Newsham, Walter Lorch, Caroline Kilford, Francesca Bryan and June Smith.

22. GLOSSARY OF COMMON TERMS

Anoestrous   a mare whose ovaries are totally inactive. The normal winter state for all mares. Can also occur when a mare is lactating.

Barren   covered but not in foal.

Breaking service   a mare comes into season again after having been covered.

Broodmare   a mare used for breeding.

Cob   a cob is a stocky, weight-carrying horse or pony. A show cob is up to 15.1 hands. Lightweight cobs can carry up to 90 kg (14 st or 196 1b) and heavyweight cobs can carry over 90 kg. A cob is a stout, thickset horse which, nevertheless, must not be ugly. Kind and willing, they are considered suitable for 'mature' riders!

Colt   a male horse of three years or less.

Corpus haemorrhagicum   the blood clot formed by the ruptured follicle at ovulation. Quickly replaced by the corpus luteum.

Corpus luteum   also known as the yellow body, it forms after ovulation and releases progesterone.

Dioestrous   the gap between two heats when a mare is not in season and the ovaries are producing progesterone.

Empty   a brood mare who was not covered.

Filly   a female horse of three years or less.

Foal   a young horse in the year of its birth.

Follicle   a swelling that develops on the ovary, containing the egg (ovum). It releases oestrogen.

FSH   follicle stimulating hormone. Produced by the pituitary gland in the brain in the early spring and throughout the breeding season. It initiates the oestrous cycle.

Gelding   a castrated male horse of any age.

Gestation   the period between conception and foaling; in practice the period from the last covering. It lasts an average of 340 days.

Hack any horse used for general riding, or a show horse of great quality and refinement. Small hacks are over 14.2 hands and up to 15 hands. Large hacks are up to 15.3 hands.

Holding a mare who has been covered and has not come into season again.

Horse can also mean the same as stallion, especially when applied to a stallion at stud (also 'full-horse', meaning not gelded).

Hunter a horse suitable for hunting. Show hunters are usually over 16 hands and categorised according to the weight of rider they can carry. Lightweight: up to 79 kg (12½ st or 175 1b); heavyweight over 90 kg (14 st or 196 1b). Middleweight in between. Small hunters are up to 15.2 hands. All hunters should have good bone and gallop well.

Hunter pony a quality pony with more bone than a riding pony, suitable for hunting.

In use Same as in season.

Lactating Producing milk for the foal.

LH Luteinizing Hormone. Produced by the pituitary gland, it triggers ovulation and the formation of corpus leuteum. Can be given artificially.

Maiden A mare who has never foaled before.

Mare A female horse of four years old or over.

Native Pony One of the nine breeds of pony that are native to the British Isles.

Oestrogen A hormone produced by follicle(s) in the ovary, which causes the mare to show by her behaviour that she is in season.

Oestrous cycle the mare's breeding cycle in the spring and summer.

Oestrus same as in season.

Ovulation the release of the egg from the follicle when it ruptures.

Oxytocin a hormone responsible for the contractions of the uterus in labour and the let-down of the milk.

Progesterone a hormone produced by the yellow body (corpus luteum) in the ovary after ovulation. It makes the mare reject the stallion.

Prostaglandin a hormone produced by a non-pregnant uterus. It 'kills' the corpus luteum so that another oestrous cycle can begin. It can also be given artificially to bring a mare into season.

Riding horse any horse that can be ridden, or a show horse intermediate in type between a hack and a hunter. Two categories: small: up to 15.2 hands; large: over 15.2.

Riding pony any pony suitable for riding, but specifically a quality pony developed in the UK mainly since the 1950s.

Rig   a gelding that behaves in many ways like a stallion, possibly because both testicles had not descended when it was gelded. A rig may be bossy with mares and aggressive towards other geldings. Do not turn a rig out with mares.

Stallion   a male horse of four years old or over.

Thoroughbred   a breed originally developed in the UK from local mares covered by Eastern (Arab) stallions and selected for speed. All racehorses are of the Thoroughbred breed, which is now found worldwide.

Warmblood   more correctly called a sports horse, this is a type developed mainly on the continent of Europe by improving heavy horses (draught and carriage types) with Arab and Thoroughbred blood. Stock is selected for its performance potential. Usually calm and easily trained.

Weaner   a weaned foal.

Weanling   same as weaner. Often applied to early foals weaned early in the latter part of their foal year.

Yearling   a young horse in the year following the year of its birth.

INDEX

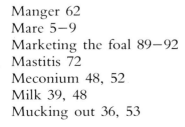

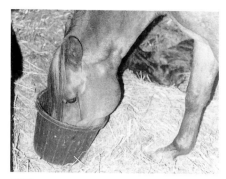

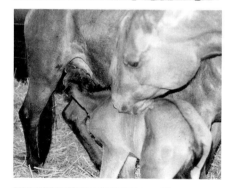